THE FORGOTTEN OFFICER

Restoring the Fullness of God's Design

JOE KOHLER

WESTBOW
PRESS®
A DIVISION OF THOMAS NELSON
& ZONDERVAN

Scripture quotations taken from the New American Standard Bible®, Copyright © 1960, 1962, 1963, 1968, 1971, 1972, 1973, 1975, 1977, 1995 by The Lockman Foundation. Used by permission. (www.Lockman.org)

WestBow Press books may be ordered through booksellers or by contacting:

WestBow Press
A Division of Thomas Nelson & Zondervan
1663 Liberty Drive
Bloomington, IN 47403
www.westbowpress.com
1 (866) 928-1240

Because of the dynamic nature of the Internet, any web addresses or links contained in this book may have changed since publication and may no longer be valid. The views expressed in this work are solely those of the author and do not necessarily reflect the views of the publisher, and the publisher hereby disclaims any responsibility for them.

Any people depicted in stock imagery provided by Thinkstock are models, and such images are being used for illustrative purposes only. Certain stock imagery © Thinkstock.

ISBN: 978-1-5127-3284-9 (sc)
ISBN: 978-1-5127-3285-6 (hc)
ISBN: 978-1-5127-3283-2 (e)

Library of Congress Control Number: 2016903723

Print information available on the last page.

WestBow Press rev. date: 4/11/2016

For the glory of God

CONTENTS

ACKNOWLEDGMENTS

I am so thankful for the support of my loving wife. I cannot adequately express the blessing you are to me, and I appreciate the sacrifices you make to allow me the time to write and minister as the Lord leads. "An excellent wife, who can find? / For her worth is far above jewels" (Prov 31:10). I have found an excellent wife and can certainly attest to your worth.

I thank all who participated in the writing of this book whether through contributing a testimony or through reading the manuscript at various stages and offering candid feedback; in several cases, it was both. To Karl, Joel, Aaron, Brian, Chris, and Tom, your contributions were a great benefit to me personally, and you have made the final work better. Finally, thank you to everyone at WestBow Press who helped bring this book into existence.

INTRODUCTION

Beloved, while I was making every effort to write you about our common salvation, I felt the necessity to write to you appealing that you contend earnestly for the faith which was once for all handed down to the saints.
—Jude 1:3

Christianity is a faith of particular content that has been handed down from the living God to the church. As Christians, our task is not to believe what we want to believe or what our itching ears want to hear. Our task as Christians is to contend earnestly for the faith handed down to the saints. We have to fight for it and cling to it. Sometimes it is obvious when we begin to deviate from biblical truth. At other times, the drift is more gradual and the truth is simply forgotten. The purpose of this book is to call attention to the role of an important but forgotten officer in the local church: the evangelist.

A popular misconception is that faith is simply belief without reason, blind faith. This may be true of some people's faith, but it is contradictory to the historical Christian faith. Biblical faith is not based on believing without reason but on believing God's promises as revealed through Scripture and through God's Son, Jesus Christ. Christian faith is built on the firm belief God will do exactly as he said he would. The historical resurrection of Jesus Christ in fulfillment of the Scriptures was proof of God's power and ability to do as he promised. Therefore, our trust, or faith, in God's Word is based on a firm foundation of God's person and his divine activity in human history.

It is foolish to be dogmatic about things that are unclear in the Scriptures. Countless divisions have arisen simply because of people's failure to be humble, to love each other, and to extend grace on ambiguous matters. In the spirit of love and unity, I don't want to fight with other Christians about our belief in the timing of Christ's return as long as we can agree that Jesus is coming back. I don't want to fight about the appropriateness of wearing jeans to a worship service or whether we are allowed to accompany our music with guitars and drums. I don't want to fight over which English translation of the Scriptures we read. My heart grieves over divisions caused by this form of disagreement on nonessentials.

When it comes to interpretation, there are seemingly always disagreements. Certainly, some of these disagreements are more important than others. The history of the professing church is filled with councils and writings fighting for the genuine faith handed down from Jesus to the apostles and endure to the present day. They fought for it because it is this revealed faith from the living God that is foundational for the church.

As a result, we can and must examine the Scriptures; we can and must examine history to see how the faith has been preserved for almost two millennia. We must also see the various shifts and trends that have emerged and influenced and continue to influence the professing church today[1] because deviations from God's revealed truth are not progress but hindrances.[2] When we allow our traditions to obscure and override the Word of God, we risk becoming modern-day Pharisees, those who look holy on the outside but inwardly are self-righteous and rebellious against the living God, nullifying God's Word with human traditions.[3]

The Word of God remains unchanging—that's the beauty of the written word![4] However, perspectives do change. It is critical for us to understand how the original recipients understood these documents if we are to rightly apply them today to our church practices and lives. Since the faith was handed down to the saints, we must maintain the original meaning and intention to rightly apply these timeless truths today; we must resist the urge to drift away from what was originally revealed.[5]

---

[1] For an excellent resource that examines the historical roots for many of our modern church practices, read Viola and Barna, *Pagan Christianity?*

[2] Prov 14:12.

[3] See, e.g., Mark 7:1–13.

[4] For those that doubt the reliability of the text that we have received, I encourage you to check out Kaiser, *Old Testament Documents*, Metzger, *Text of the New Testament*, and Geisler, *Systematic Theology*, 1:229–563.

[5] Heb 2:1–4.

One of the first textbooks I was assigned in seminary related to the task of rightly handling the Scriptures. It was a helpful book that taught a high view of rightly understanding the written Word as it was originally intended and an appreciation of how the church has interpreted the Word throughout history. As a result of these priorities, it states in the introductory chapter, "Let it be said at the outset—and repeated throughout—that the aim of good interpretation is not uniqueness; one is not trying to discover what no one else has ever seen before. … Unique interpretations are usually wrong."[6] This is wise counsel.

Jesus, Paul, Peter, John, Jude, and the author of Hebrews all warned of the danger of false teachers among professing Christians.[7] Many of these teachers offer unique interpretations of the Scriptures and claim their spiritual attainments or special positions with the Lord have granted them the ability to unlock these deep spiritual mysteries for those who follow them. Unique interpretations are a good way to breed division and are essential for starting cults.

These unique interpretations of Scripture are often tailored to a particular audience or are the result of a particular bias of the interpreter(s). They are aimed either at convincing followers who want these things to be true or are claimed by those who want them to be true themselves. Unique interpretations sell books. Unique interpretations can create followings. At least, popular ones can.

Some think the interpretation of Ephesians 4:11–16 presented in this book is unique. I do know one thing for sure: it is not popular. If I wanted to start a cult or create a following, this would not be the place to do it. I once heard a pastor ask his congregation during a sermon, "At what point do I cross the line and step on your toes? At what point do I cross the line from good preaching to meddling?" This is a fair question. The rhetorical point was that this hypothetical line was in different places for everyone.

Almost everyone has a line drawn when it comes to personal evangelism and gospel witnessing. Experience has shown me that this line is quickly crossed when I affirm that the Scriptures tell us Jesus's design for his church requires

---

[6] Fee and Stuart, *How to Read the Bible*, 17–18.
[7] E.g., Matt 7:15–29; Acts 20:28–30; 2 Cor 11:13–15; 2 Pet 2:1–22; 1 John 4:1; Jude 1:3–4; Heb 13:9.

all Christians to be equipped and faithful in the ministry of reconciliation as ambassadors in Christ's kingdom or else we are not fully mature.[8]

Most professing Christians I've encountered are comfortable with the idea that evangelists are the professionals in the work of evangelizing the lost or are specially gifted for this task. Many are even excited to sow in the ministries of these professionals and to hear the exciting stories from out in the field.

Yet experience has also demonstrated that it is crossing the line for many of these same professing Christians to claim that biblically speaking, evangelists exist to equip them personally for evangelizing the world and that evangelism is not something that can be farmed out to the "professionals"![9] I have witnessed their irritation directly.

Some could (and do) argue that this interpretation of Ephesians 4:11–16 is unique and therefore probably wrong. The same book that teaches unique interpretations are usually wrong continues, however, to say, "This is not to say that the correct understanding of a text may not often seem unique to someone who hears it for the first time. But it is to say that uniqueness is *not* the aim of our task."[10] And uniqueness is not the aim of my task.

As a teacher of God's Word, my task is to be faithful to the living God and his revelation. Related to this pursuit is the task of not allowing the body of Christ to be conformed to the ways of this world (which includes infusing biblical terminology with new meanings based on our culture instead of the text). We must allow our minds to be renewed and transformed by the Word of God.[11] With these tasks in mind, I have written this book because I believe the church in the United States has drifted from the truth of Ephesians 4:11–16 in theory and practice. As a result of its drifting away, we are now in a position where hearing the plain meaning of this text explained and exposed seems unique because we are hearing it for the first time.

What is comforting for me is that every aspect of the interpretation of Ephesians 4:11–16 in this book is already represented in the writings of commentators, scholars, and other Christian leaders. This means that this

---

[8] 2 Cor 5:17–21; Eph 4:12–16. More on this in chapter 1.

[9] This claim is developed in much more detail in chapters 8 and 9.

[10] Fee and Stuart, *How to Read the Bible*, 18, italics in original.

[11] Rom 12:2.

interpretation is actually not unique even if it is uncommon among actual leadership structures in our churches. The unique aspect of the model presented in these pages is how it all comes together and in the resulting application to the body of Christ.

Are you ever amazed at the Pharisees and scribes when you read the Gospels? While often thought of as the villains by many Christians, these guys were serious about the Scriptures. A big part of their problem was that they nullified the Word of God with their human traditions.[12] As a result of their knowledge of the Word of God, Jesus often responded to them by saying, "Have you not read?"[13] Of course, Jesus knew they had read the Scriptures; they had just allowed their traditions to nullify what had been written.

Perhaps even more amazing is how often modern-day followers of Jesus scoff at the foolishness of the Pharisees while doing the same thing. Our denominational traditions are powerful, as is the way we use language. We are not immune from infusing biblical words with our own definitions and reading our new definitions (not the original intended meaning) into the text.[14] Changing the definitions of words and shifting our terminology can have dramatic effects. For example, when we change the terminology of human beings in the womb from *baby* to *fetus*, the jump to *choice* is more acceptable. *Procedure* is easier to handle when discussing an abortion than *murder*. Words are powerful. When we infuse biblical terms with our own meanings, we are in grave danger of nullifying the Word of God with our own traditions. We have to at least admit the possibility that we can nullify the Word of God with the traditions we have made for ourselves. Other traditions we have simply inherited.

There are a number of different interpretations regarding the role of evangelists in the church, but none of the most popular does the biblical witness justice.[15] We can't all be right.[16] Modern culture has taken a biblical

---

[12] Mark 7:13.

[13] E.g., Matt 12:3–5; 19:4; 22:31.

[14] The technical name for this practice is *eisegesis*.

[15] This claim will be demonstrated in much greater detail in chapter 8.

[16] For a good discussion on the nature of truth, a demonstration that all truth is absolute, and a strong refutation of relativism, see Geisler, *Systematic Theology*, 1:109–25.

word and infused it with new definitions. Sadly, the term *evangelist* has shifted toward antibiblical meanings. Our cultural redefining of the biblical term has caused us to be blind to what the text plainly says.

It is in the spirit of love that I gently ask the church regarding Ephesians 4:11–16, "Have you not read?"

My humble hope is that in these pages I will help the church rediscover what has been forgotten. In particular, I make the case for the inclusion of evangelists among the plurality of elders in the local church government as a biblical norm. Some have objected that it is improper to attempt to say there is an "office" of evangelist because there are only two offices in the church: elders and deacons. Of course, not everyone holds to the two-office view. Perhaps the most difficult issue to overcome regarding discussion on the biblical role of evangelists is due to terminology since no matter what words we use, someone will take issue. Despite the difficulty of terminology, I urge you to stick with me until the end before drawing your conclusions. The truth is worth fighting for.

God's Word can declare the right path for us and predict the problems that await us when we stray. Taking a closer look at the importance of this matter will demonstrate that the present situation in the church could have been predicted as a result of our wandering from Christ's design for his church. The bad news is that the consequences are real, but the good news is that Scripture does not leave us in the dark—it lights the path forward.[17] Scripture is profitable for teaching us what is right, for reproving us when we stray, for correcting our course, and for training us in righteousness.[18] Praise God that by his grace we can regain the glorious design of his church and walk in the fullness of Christ!

---

[17] Ps 119:105.
[18] 2 Tim 3:16–17.

CHAPTER 1

Fullness by Design

And He gave some as apostles, and some as prophets, and some as evangelists, and some as pastors and teachers, for the equipping of the saints for the work of service, to the building up of the body of Christ; until we all attain to the unity of the faith, and of the knowledge of the Son of God, to a mature man, to the measure of the stature which belongs to the fullness of Christ.
—Ephesians 4:11–13

Culture is powerful. We have all inherited a culture, but we often fail to evaluate it. Instead, we often take our particular culture for granted and celebrate it. But what if it is not worthy of celebration? Are we willing to discard it or at least its harmful parts?

The apostle Peter wrote to followers of Jesus Christ scattered throughout Pontus, Galatia, Cappadocia, Asia, and Bithynia,

> If you address as Father the One who impartially judges according to each one's work, conduct yourselves in fear during the time of your stay on earth; knowing that you were not redeemed with perishable things like silver or gold from your futile way of life inherited from your forefathers, but with precious blood, as of a lamb unblemished and spotless, the blood of Christ. (1 Pet 1:17–19)

Peter taught them they had been redeemed from the way of life they had inherited from their forebearers. Writing under the inspiration of the Holy Spirit, Peter had no problem calling inherited cultures futile, no exceptions or qualifications. He categorized every inherited way of life as something that needed to be discarded. Peter's expectation was that Christians would live as aliens in the midst of their geographical regions. Inherited culture was part of what Jesus died to redeem his people from.

When Peter addressed these believers residing across the Greco-Roman Empire, he called them "aliens."[19] This word in 1 Peter 1:11 is translated as "exiles" (ESV), "strangers" (KJV), "sojourners" (NAB), "those temporarily residing abroad" (NET), and "strangers in the world" (NIV). Despite the variety of translations, the idea remains constant: they were residents of the kingdom of heaven and therefore lived as temporary visitors in whatever country or region they resided.[20] While this may seem like a relatively common concept in Christianity, the implications of such teaching from Peter are often skewed.

If our teaching and preaching merely focus the attention of the believer on the reality that we are citizens of heaven who will one day dwell with our God, we have missed the point of Peter's writing this epistle. Peter returned to this theme in the next chapter: "Beloved, I urge you as aliens and strangers to abstain from fleshly lusts which wage war against the soul" (1 Pet 2:11). Peter was applying the great theological truth of our heavenly citizenship to the present lives of the follower of Christ, not simply giving them hope for the future. If our citizenship is genuinely in heaven, that fact should have profound implications on our current lives and lifestyles.

Some strands of preaching and teaching emphasize the importance of Christians being "normal" and looking like the rest of the culture so that they have some common ground to discuss the Christian faith with those who do not attend church. The apostle Peter was teaching something that disagreed with this notion.[21] Christians must be in the world and must interact with it, but they must not conform to the world or be of it. Peter instructed Christians to live

> as obedient children, [and] do not be conformed to the former lusts which were yours in ignorance, but like the Holy One who called you, be holy yourselves in all your behavior, because it is written, "You shall be holy, for I am holy." (1 Pet 1:14–16)

---

[19] Gk: παρεπίδημος (parepidēmos).

[20] Cf. Phil 3:20.

[21] James also strongly disagrees with this modern idea; see Jas 4:4.

Peter thought that the way of life we inherited before we were brought to new life in Jesus Christ was futile;[22] his encouragement to followers of Christ was not to continue in futility and conformity to the former lusts of their flesh due to their ignorance of God and his ways. Peter warned that the false teachers would teach us to continue to live this way.[23] Instead, Peter encouraged us to come out from such foolishness. The old, familiar ways of life should become stranger and stranger to us. Christians are called to replace their futile, worldly culture and way of life they inherited with a heavenly culture and way of life given by Christ. This heavenly culture is by nature abnormal and foreign to the world.

Instead of encouraging us to embrace the culture and the futile way of life inherited from our forebearers, Peter was calling us to live as aliens and strangers in this world so we would not be distracted from advancing the glory of God, our calling. This is exactly what he wrote in 1 Peter 2:9–10.

Peter's model looks very different from the "blending in" model that is comfortable for our flesh. Instead of looking like the world, Peter called us to look and live differently. In fact, for Peter, this was much more noticeable to the surrounding culture. When I was in Ethiopia, I stuck out like a sore thumb. It was not just because of my skin color; my clothes, language, style, activities—everything about me—screamed "alien and stranger," but I could not help it. Peter called for Christians to embrace this as a lifestyle because the culture we have inherited (no matter where it came from) was futile, if it were not directly from Christ and the kingdom of heaven.

Some believe that being familiar with popular culture will make it easier to have conversations with worldly people, but what is the value in discussing what celebrities are dating whom or what sports teams are competing for some title? Do we think we will spend any time in heaven discussing such trivialities? Do we not realize that clothing ourselves in the garb of a futile world culture is a walk in futility?

Those who teach that Christians should blend in with the culture sometimes want non-Christians to see that followers of Christ are not really that different from the rest of the world. Peter taught exactly the opposite: that genuine followers of Christ were supposed to live entirely different

---

[22] Compare this to Paul's statements in Rom 8:20–21 and Eph 4:17–24.
[23] 2 Pet 2:1—3:18.

from the rest of the world and be aliens and strangers to everything that is relevant, important, and popular to the world. If you are not from here, how could you know about the popular culture? Christians have been called out of darkness and into light and ought to walk as children of light.

In Ephesians 2, Paul wrote that when we walked according to the course of this world, we were God's enemies—aliens and strangers to his kingdom. Now that we have been forgiven of our sins and brought into the family of God, we are citizens of heaven and should no longer walk in death but in life. These two lifestyles are very different. Paul summarized his application on this theme. In Ephesians 5:7–17, he once again encouraged Christians to no longer participate in the deeds of darkness and walk in futility but to walk in wisdom and light because the days are evil.

Being all things to everyone does not include walking as a dead person in the futile culture we have inherited from our forebearers. Paul sought to minister to Gentile as well as Jew, two radically different cultures; he strove to not be offensive to the people he was ministering to by violating their cultural views of certain things. That does not mean he participated in everything they participated in. While I was in Ethiopia, it was important that I knew which hand to eat with because of particular customs relating to sanitation that would have been offensive if I had violated them, but it was not important to become an expert on their sports teams and popular culture.

The author of Hebrews picked up this same terminology when writing of the faithfulness of some of the saints of the past.

> All these died in faith, without receiving the promises, but having seen them and having welcomed them from a distance, and having confessed that they were strangers and exiles on the earth. For those who say such things make it clear that they are seeking a country of their own. And indeed if they had been thinking of that country from which they went out, they would have had opportunity to return. But as it is, they desire a better country, that is, a heavenly one. Therefore God is not ashamed to be called their God; for He has prepared a city for them. (Heb 11:13–16)

Here we find the term Peter used in 1 Peter 1:1 translated as "exiles" and paired with a much more commonly used word in the New Testament translated as "strangers."[24] A survey of the usage of this term really emphasizes that *strangers* means something similar to *outsiders.*

In stark contrast to teachers that emphasize looking like the world, Peter, Paul, and the author of Hebrews emphasized that the faith worthy of being lived by followers of Christ would appear very strange to those who were part of the futile culture of the dead, dark world. Those of us who have been awakened from spiritual death and redeemed from the penalty and power of our sin should grow in our understanding of God and the futility of the ways of this world.

The grace of God in the lives of us, his children, should always be working toward conforming us to the image of his Son.[25] God should constantly be making us more and more aware of aspects of our flesh that need to be put to death by the Spirit.[26]

We must not twist the Scriptures or the grace of God into covering for our continuing in sin and walking according to the lusts of our flesh and in the ways of this world.[27] When Paul claimed that he became all things to all people so he could save some, he also stated in the next verse that he did all things for the sake of the gospel.[28] Paul made these statements in the face of accusations that were being made of him and challenges to his genuine status as an apostle. Paul was laying down his rights through the exercise of his Christian liberty so he would have no opportunity to offend those he ministered to. Paul was not participating in anything that might have caused some to stumble—meaning this passage cannot be used to condone drinking with your buddies at the bar or watching godless entertainment that glorifies worldliness, covetousness, and sexual immorality because those things do cause people to stumble.[29] If you abstain from such activities, even if it may be okay for you to do them in

---

[24] Gk. ξένος (*xenos*). This word occurs fourteen times in the New Testament: Matt 25:35, 38, 43–44; 27:7; Acts 17:18, 21; Rom 16:23; Eph 2:12, 19; Heb 11:13; 13:9; 1 Pet 4:12; and 3 John 1:5.

[25] Rom 8:29.

[26] Rom 8:13–14.

[27] Rom 6:1–23; 1 Pet 2:16; 2 Pet 3:14–18.

[28] 1 Cor 9:22–23.

[29] Eph 5:5–6; 1 Cor 6:9–11.

moderation because you are not saved by your works but by the grace of God, it is possible people will slander you just as they did Paul.[30]

The biblical testimony is clear and consistent: followers of Christ are not called to be conformed to the patterns and ways of the world[31] but to live as aliens and strangers because they have been redeemed from the futile ways of life they inherited.[32] This is true regardless of the particular form of dead culture they were rescued from.[33]

We Christians are called to live holy in this world as citizens of the kingdom of heaven.[34] We must constantly be aware of the war that wages against our souls and keep our focus on Jesus, the author and perfecter of our faith.[35]

Teachings that encourage Christians to embrace the culture are dangerous. Read carefully the words of James: "You adulteresses, do you not know that friendship with the world is hostility toward God? Therefore whoever wishes to be a friend of the world makes himself an enemy of God" (Jas 4:4). The language he uses is vivid and strong. Continuing to be friends with the world is adultery toward the God who called us to be a holy people for him. It is a deception that we can be friends of God and the world at the same time; when we try to be friends with the world, we live as God's enemies.

If we love the things of this world and the dead expressions of culture, the apostle John likewise has stern words for us: "Do not love the world nor the things in the world. If anyone loves the world, the love of the Father is not in him" (1 John 2:15). For John—the beloved disciple, one of the members of the inner circle of Jesus's disciples, and the one who reclined on Jesus at the Last Supper[36]—it is simple: if you love the world, you do not love the Father.[37]

Of course it must be stated clearly that to live as strangers is not

---

[30] See also 1 Pet 2:12.

[31] Rom 12:1–2.

[32] 1 Pet 1:17–19, 2:11; Heb 11:13.

[33] Eph 2:1–3; 1 Pet 1:18.

[34] Eph 2:19; Phil 3:17–21.

[35] 2 Cor 10:3–6; Eph 6:10–20; Heb 12:1–11; 1 Pet 2:11.

[36] John 13:25; 21:20.

[37] Those interested in an excellent exposition of the message of 1 John and the assurance that Christians can have of their salvation (in addition to the warnings

necessarily a call to live strangely. There is a difference between being an alien and being a weirdo. When we begin to die to the things of this world and live for the things of God, our lifestyle will definitely seem strange to the world—but for the right reasons. It will not be strange for the same reasons that some people have reality television shows about themselves.

A simple life in the midst of decadence is strange. A life of self-control in a world filled with self-indulgence is strange. A life of purity in the midst of a world filled with immorality is strange. A life that values those whom society deems worthless is strange. A life that blesses enemies and prays for those who persecute us in the midst of a world that slanders and seeks self-interest above all else is strange.

A life built around proclaiming the gospel of Jesus Christ to the ends of the earth in obedience to the command of the risen King will be strange in a world filled with rebels against that King who live to fulfill their fleshly lusts and impulses.

We do not have to go beyond simple godliness to add additional odd behaviors in our attempt to be "different;" living godly in a godless world is different enough.

If you are a Christian, you are called to live for the purposes and glory of God as an alien and a stranger on earth. Living for the purposes of God includes proclaiming the excellencies of God, who has called us out of darkness and into light to be a people for him.[38]

This world is not your home. As the grace of God continues to conform you more and more to the image of Jesus, you should become more and more uncomfortable here. Children of God should long more deeply to be in the undiluted presence of the living God. If you are comfortable in this present world and love the culture, the Bible warns you that you are living as God's enemy and lovingly calls you to repentance and life in the Savior.

This world is dead and under God's curse.[39] As a result, when we conform ourselves to the patterns of this world, we are walking in death. In contrast, Christ has called his followers to abundant life.[40] In light of

---

that false professions of Christ must hear from Matt 7:13–27) are encouraged to read Paul Washer's excellent book *Gospel Assurance & Warnings*.

[38] 1 Pet 2:9–11.

[39] Gen 3. For more on this see Kohler, *Gate Crashers*, 1–34.

[40] John 10:10.

the biblical testimony, this does not mean Jesus is calling us to be filled up with the things this world says are important. Instead, he calls us to know him and be known by him.[41] That is genuine life.

Our culture is inherited; instead of being part of our genetics, we assimilate our culture by growing up in it rather than inheriting it the way we do eye color. If an Asian baby and an African baby are switched, they will grow up with physiological traits based on their genetics, but their cultures will be based on where they grow up.

If you are a Christian, you were born again into the kingdom of heaven. Your citizenship and spiritual genetics now make you a child of God. However, you have acquired a worldly culture by being a part of the world for so long. The biblical plan for acquiring the new, heavenly culture is likewise to grow up in it.[42]

I want my six young children to grow up to full maturity.[43] That's not to say I want to skip past all the fun things that accompany young kids. In fact, as each day passes I realize how quickly these moments go by. But the march to adulthood is inevitable. My children are growing up whether I like it or not. But maturity is not the same as age; it is possible to get older while never really growing up.

I want my children to realize their potential and grow to be responsible adults. I don't want my three sons to live in my house indefinitely, expecting their mother to cook and clean for them when they are in their thirties and forties. It is reasonable to spoon-feed infants but not adult sons and daughters.

Part of my responsibility as a father is to steward the children God has so graciously given us so they can be delivered safely into maturity. As Christians, we have a heavenly Father who likewise desires that we grow to full maturity in Christ. As is the case with our natural growth, spiritual maturity is not the same as spiritual age. We are not necessarily more mature simply because we have been Christians for a long time. To think that maturity and age are the same is wrong.

In Ephesians 5:17, the apostle Paul wrote, "So then do not be foolish,

---

[41] John 17:3.

[42] E.g., 2 Pet 3:18.

[43] The rest of this chapter is a modified version of a blog article originally published on our ministry website: www.fourthyearministries.com.

but understand what the will of the Lord is." This is good counsel. To understand what Paul meant about the will of the Lord, we must understand what he had written about in Ephesians—God's will that the church reach full maturity for the praise and glory of his name. This fullness doesn't come by accident or simply by passing the time; it comes by walking according to God's design.

Ephesians 1 is filled with some of the deepest theology you will find in the Bible. It touches on the work of the triune God in redeeming a people for himself from the world, which is the same thing Peter was talking about in his first epistle. Ephesians 1 discusses the Father's plan to choose a people for himself from before the foundation of the world to be holy and blameless before him (Eph 1:3–4). It tells of God's predetermined plan to adopt us into his family through Christ to the praise of the glory of his grace (Eph 1:5–6). And it tells us God made known to us his plan and revealed the mystery of his will he purposed in Christ with a view to an administration suitable to the fullness of the times, that is, the summing up of all things in Christ (Eph 1:9–10).

That last part is so important to really understand. The word translated as *administration* in the NASB is the Greek word οἰκονομία (*oikonomia*), which appears here in 1:10 and twice more in Ephesians (3:2 and 3:9). This word refers to a sphere of influence to be managed or a state of arrangement.[44] This is seen in the common translation as "stewardship," "dispensation," or "plan." Though translators are somewhat split on the best way to render this term in English (as a survey of the modern English renderings of Eph 1:10, 3:2, and 3:9 will show), when we follow Paul's thought, we see that God was overseeing a plan and putting people in charge of various spheres to bring that plan to completion. God is sovereign over the whole plan of redeeming a people to himself from every tribe, tongue, and nation and unifying them in Christ, and God entrusts a stewardship (a management or oversight position) to individuals to participate in this plan of salvation.

God had a plan before he made the world to redeem a people for himself in and through Christ to be for the praise of his glory (Eph 1:12). The existence of the redeemed people of God (the church)—our very being—is supposed to bring glory to God's amazing, transformative,

---

[44] See particularly the first two entries for οἰκονομία in BDAG.

and redemptive grace he has so lavishly and freely bestowed on us in Christ.

God then made known the mystery of his will so we who have been adopted into his family would understand what he was doing in the world and in the church. In fact, Paul explained his personal ministry in the following way.

> If indeed you have heard of the stewardship [οἰκονομία] of God's grace which was given to me for you; that by revelation there was made known to me the mystery, as I wrote before in brief. By referring to this, when you read you can understand my insight into the mystery of Christ, which in other generations was not made known to the sons of men, as it has now been revealed to His holy apostles and prophets in the Spirit; to be specific, that the Gentiles are fellow heirs and fellow members of the body, and fellow partakers of the promise in Christ Jesus through the gospel, of which I was made a minister, according to the gift of God's grace which was given to me according to the working of His power. To me, the very least of all saints, this grace was given, to preach to the Gentiles the unfathomable riches of Christ, and to bring to light what is the administration [οἰκονομία] of the mystery which for ages has been hidden in God who created all things; so that the manifold wisdom of God might now be made known through the church to the rulers and the authorities in the heavenly places. This was in accordance with the eternal purpose which He carried out in Christ Jesus our Lord. (Eph 3:2–11)

God has a plan and the means to achieve it. He has given grace to achieve his goals and has designed an administration suitable to the fullness of the times, the summing up of all things in Christ (Eph 1:10). This administration points to God's gracious oversight of the process of transforming dead sinners into living saints who will be for the praise of God's glorious grace. This is essentially the topic of Ephesians 2.

Right before discussing God's transformative, redemptive grace in chapter 2, Paul made an astonishing statement at the end of chapter 1: "And He put all things in subjection under His feet, and gave Him as head over all things to the church, which is His body, the fullness of Him who fills all in all" (Eph 1:22–23). Sometimes, I hear professing Christians say disparaging things about the church. We should be very careful with such statements. By divine design, the church is Christ's body on earth and the fullness of him who fills all in all.

Let that sink in: the genetics of the church is the fullness of Christ, who fills all in all. If what we perceive and observe as the church does not fit this description, we are looking at the wrong thing or failing to walk in the grace God has given because we've attempted to redesign God's church and are walking in human traditions that have nullified his Word. Paul's expectation of God's working through his glorious church was extremely high.

> Now to Him who is able to do far more abundantly beyond all that we ask or think, according to the power that works within us, to Him be the glory in the church and in Christ Jesus to all generations forever and ever. Amen. (Eph 3:20–21)

If what we have inherited or made ourselves in our church culture is contrary to the genetics of God's design, we must throw off and resist it; otherwise, it would hinder God's perfect purposes from being fulfilled in his church.

Since God had a plan and a design, since he had made his will known, and since he had already put all things in subjection under Christ, Paul had no problem asserting that God's power was at work in us to bring himself glory in the church and in Christ Jesus for all generations, forever and ever.

This is awesome stuff. It also requires responsibility on our end as God's adopted children. This is why in the next sentence Paul wrote, "Therefore I, the prisoner of the Lord, implore you to walk in a manner worthy of the calling with which you have been called" (Eph 4:1). Paul implored the saints to understand the will of the Lord and to walk in a worthy way, according to God's grace and design. It is in this line of thought in Ephesians 4 where Paul described most fully the administration that God designed and gave by his grace for the growth of the body into the fullness of Christ. Just as a child is born with a genetic identity but must grow into maturity, so the church is by genetic identity the fullness of Christ but must also grow up into this identity.

God has a design and a will he has made known. He wants the church to be the fullness of Jesus, who fills all in all. He entrusted Paul with a stewardship of grace to proclaim this design (Eph 3:1–10) of God's administration, which is given to bring about the full maturity of the body.

Paul wrote that each member had received grace (Eph 4:7) and that the risen Jesus gave officials to the whole body to equip the saints "until we all attain to the unity of the faith, and of the knowledge of the Son of God, *to a mature man, to the measure of the stature which belongs to the fullness of Christ*" (Eph 4:13, emphasis added). These officers are the apostles, prophets, evangelists, pastors, and teachers given to help the body grow into the maturity and stature appropriate for the church, namely, the fullness of Christ.

Fullness, maturity, doesn't happen by accident but by the grace of God. It happens by the body of Christ understanding the will of the Lord and submitting itself to Christ's design to the praise of his grace. We must walk in a manner worthy of our calling.

Without the apostles and prophets—the foundation (Eph 2:18—3:10)—we would have no idea what God's divine will was. Thankfully, God revealed the mystery of his will through his apostles and prophets, and we have this revelation in the Scriptures. These are the very terms the apostle Paul used when writing the letter to the saints at Ephesus and describing his ministry as an apostle. As Christians, we must submit ourselves to the biblical revelation, which is where the apostles and prophets have been preserved. The book of Ephesians is a part of this apostolic foundation.

If we survey the body of Christ, we see many pastors and teachers who exist for the equipping of the saints in every church. They teach, shepherd, and oversee the fellowship of believers (built upon the apostolic and prophetic foundation) and are critically important to the health of the body.

However, one element of the administration given by Christ is conspicuously absent in the vast majority of local churches: the evangelists.

We must not make the mistake of thinking that simply because we have inherited church structures that omit the biblical function and role of evangelists in the permanent local church leadership that this was not part of the original genetic code and God's design for his church.

The modern idea of evangelists we have inherited has primarily pushed them out into parachurch ministry and redefined them as ministers to the lost and revivalist-type preachers who stir up the body on special occasions. But the apostolic foundation says that Christ gave these officers for the equipping of the saints, not for the reaching of the lost.

The whole church, not just the evangelists, exists to reach the lost and make disciples. Every member is important and must be equipped to function properly for building up the whole body.[45]

We have pushed out evangelists to the fringe (at best) of the church; it is no wonder many think the church falls short of Paul's lofty comments. We have strayed from the intended design and as a result are walking foolishly in the futile way of life we have inherited. We are walking according to human designs, not according to the fullness of God's revealed administration for bringing about our maturity in the body of Christ.

By the grace of God, we can understand what the will of the Lord is and can once again walk wisely in his gracious plan and according to his power, which is at work in us.

Chris—A Testimony

(Chris, a controls engineer, personally and regularly shares the gospel with hundreds to thousands of individuals each year.)

Prior to serving under church leadership that included an evangelist, I lived what I considered a typical Christian life for someone in the American church. I would read my Bible often, pray daily, attend church on Sunday, and enroll in occasional Bible study courses.

My Christian walk was quiet and personal; I never really plugged myself into my church community. I did not know many people nor did I make much of an effort to get to know people. I didn't spend any time outside of the church building talking to friends or family about Jesus

---

[45] Eph 4:14–16. See also Kohler, *Gate Crashers*, chapter 5.

either. My faith was my thing; my way of sharing my faith was to live the best example of the Christian life I could be without talking to anyone about Jesus. This was (and still is) the example I see in many American Christians today.

However, things started to change once our church hired a full-time evangelist; prior to that, our church had only pastors. While our senior pastor always made sure to preach biblical messages that focused on the need to share the gospel with friends, coworkers, family, relatives—everyone on earth—there was never anyone in place to hold the body accountable to share the gospel and to lead this charge full-time. The pastor preached it and taught classes on it, but he had other duties.

I remember feeling convicted by the Holy Spirit that I should be intentional about sharing the gospel with others each week after hearing the sermon. However, nobody was personally holding me accountable to do so. Once I left the church building, the conviction would gradually go away and I would return to my normal habits until the next Sunday.

Additionally, at that time, my understanding of evangelism was inaccurate and unbiblical. I viewed evangelism as a spiritual gift given only to some (and certainly not to me). I also thought evangelists were more or less the same thing as missionaries. While I supported the idea of evangelism and sharing the gospel, I didn't think it was something for me to do as an individual. I thought my role in evangelism was limited to supporting missionaries financially and living out my life as a Christian without actually opening my mouth to share the gospel with anyone. I am a giver; I had been taught wrongly that giving to evangelism and supporting the work of those doing evangelism was enough. Now I know I can do both.

Our evangelist brought accountability to the congregation in the realm of evangelism because he was devoted fully to this cause, not having to try to balance the duties of a pastor and an evangelist which can often be too difficult for one person to handle alone. I remember the evangelist creating and sharing videos with the congregation about the need to share the gospel, having others give testimony about sharing the gospel, and inviting us to go out and intentionally share our faith in the community with him. Having this and the biblical truths preached every week by the pastor brought about in me even more conviction from the Holy Spirit.

Only that time, the conviction did not go away once I left the church building; it stayed with me throughout the week, and I began to be more concerned with the reality that I was not living in obedience to God.

Even though I was feeling conviction from the Holy Spirit and agreed I was being disobedient to the Lord, I still did not submit to Him by sharing the gospel with others. Instead, I hid behind the fear I had and the excuses I made. Then one day, the evangelist contacted me about his plan to form a group of disciples who would meet once a week to read the Bible though the lens of evangelism. I thought it would be a good opportunity to get to know the evangelist and to further my knowledge of evangelism.

The first class was a very humbling experience. Our evangelist spoke boldly and truthfully about the command to go and make disciples, a command I was not obeying. For the first time, I had to deal with my disobedience by not sharing the gospel.

That Bible study shed light on two major personal problems. First, my thought that sharing the gospel was optional for me (or, for anyone who claims to be a Christian) was not a biblical truth. Sharing the gospel is not optional; it is a command.

Second, I did not understand what the gospel really was nor did I understand how to share it biblically. Thankfully, one of the main functions of the evangelist is to train and equip people to share the gospel in a biblically faithful way. Therefore, the evangelist enrolled me in multiple classes to teach me what the gospel was and how to effectively share it. His teaching challenged me in ways I had never been challenged before since I was always a quiet Christian who had kept to myself. Sharing the gospel required me to be bold and to actually open my mouth.

To say that I am a shy person is an understatement. I did not have many friends growing up; since I was not popular in school, I tried to make myself as unnoticeable as possible. Because I am a soft-spoken person who does not enjoy approaching strangers or meeting new people, the idea of approaching strangers to share the gospel terrified me. At first, I thought there was no way I would be able to participate in this command.

I was so scared the first time I went out with our evangelist to witness. We met downtown and went out together. At first, I just observed and listened to him go through the gospel with numerous people. Then he informed me it was my turn. I was more than nervous, but with his and the Holy Spirit's help, I was able to faithfully and fully share the gospel for the first time.

Did it go perfectly? No. Did I stumble at times? Yes. But when I got done, for the first time in my eight years of professing Christ as my Lord and Savior, I felt I was alive in Christ. Before I started witnessing, I was on Christianity's sidelines; I wasn't an active member of the body of Christ because I wasn't out there working to advance his kingdom so he would receive glory, honor, and praise. Instead, I was a lazy and disobedient Christian unwilling to be used by God for one of the main purposes he created me for.

The impact the evangelist has had on me was very significant to my growth as a Christian. Without him, my Christian walk would have been severely hindered. Before I sat under the authority of our evangelist, I thought that sharing the gospel was only for those who had the gift. I even thought witnessing was only a minor part of being a Christian. However, sharing the gospel affects and shapes every aspect of my Christian walk. Because I am obedient in witnessing, I have a better understanding of the Bible, which has improved my study habits and my ability to teach the Bible to others.

Witnessing has also improved my prayer life. I am now able to pray more in line with God's will. My prayer life is no longer my personal wish list to God about things I want. Also, my participation in the other spiritual disciplines such as fasting, meditation,[46] and worship has improved. I find myself participating more often in these disciplines and growing in Christ because of it.

Finally, my love and compassion for others, especially the lost, has grown exponentially. Before I sat under the authority of an evangelist, I didn't have a good understanding of what the gospel was or even how to go about sharing it. On top of that, I did not feel alive in Christ; I felt as if I were asleep. I'm not saying I wasn't saved, but I was spiritually immature. I was not fully participating in the calling Christ gives to all who call him Lord and Savior. If it wasn't for the evangelist, I would have never received

---

[46] Christian meditation is vastly different from Eastern forms of meditation, which cause the practitioner to attempt to empty their minds. Instead, in Christian meditation, the mind is filled with God's Word and works. E.g., Ps 119:15.

the necessary training to go out and share the gospel. Now, because of our evangelist, I find myself sharing the gospel daily.

I don't share this testimony to boast about what I am doing for the Lord but because God calls us to do it, partners with us in this work, and promises to be with us while we are out spreading the good news. Because of this, why wouldn't we share the only message that can save people from the wrath of God and allow them to enjoy his love and grace forever?

CHAPTER 2

Inheritance, Reform, and Revival

If you address as Father the One who impartially judges according to each one's work, conduct yourselves in fear during the time of your stay on earth; knowing that you were not redeemed with perishable things like silver or gold from your futile way of life inherited from your forefathers, but with precious blood, as of a lamb unblemished and spotless, the blood of Christ.
—1 Peter 1:17–19

We have not simply inherited a culture from the world; the church has a culture that has been passed from generation to generation. If we are not careful to cling to the faith handed down to the saints, we risk creating a way of life that is church flavored but is still just as futile as the world's culture. In some cases, the church-flavored culture is more dangerous because we can be deceived into believing everything is fine when it is not.[47]

In our modern church setting, we have inherited a leadership model that strays from the apostolic foundation described in Ephesians 4:11–16. To maintain a healthy culture, the apostle Paul passed down traditions that were supposed to be held firmly by the church.[48]

Some denominations take these traditions seriously, but it seems other denominations delight in creating new cultures for the church devoid of symbolism from and attachment to the church from previous ages. Separating from the historical faith is like trying to erect a roof with no

---

[47] The *many* referred to in Matt 7:21–23 comes to mind.
[48] 1 Cor 11:1–2; 2 Thess 2:15.

walls.[49] We must be careful to walk the narrow path between the extremes of simply holding to traditions that nullify the Word of God and the opposite error of discarding all tradition and attempting to interpret the Scriptures in a vacuum, separated from the life of the church from the beginning.

The apostle Paul affirmed that the Old Testament writings were written for our instruction and edification.[50] We can learn from the history of God's people in the past to see how we ought to walk with the living God today. This does not mean we are to take the Law upon ourselves or try to recreate what God was doing through Israel. Attempting to take the Law upon ourselves is an error the apostles dealt directly with in Acts 15, Colossians, and Galatians. However, since there is nothing new under the sun, we can learn from Israel's mistakes and attempt to be faithful where it fell.[51] In this regard, the history recorded in the Old Testament is helpful and instructive.

God promised to make of Abram a great nation;[52] he brought Abram to the land that would one day be the territory this nation would possess and began to fulfill his promise through Isaac and Isaac's son, Jacob.

Joseph, one of Jacob's twelve sons, fulfilled a special purpose in being sent ahead of the rest of the clan into Egypt, where he rose to great power as second only to Pharaoh. Through revelation and wisdom given to Joseph, a plan was implemented that saved many lives during a severe famine, but it resulted in the consolidation of power and people into the hands of the Egyptians.[53] God allowed the clan of Jacob to remain in the land of Goshen for 430 years, where they grew in population from about seventy to a great multitude—about 600,000 men aside from women and children.[54]

God raised up Moses to deliver his people out of Egypt. God led them into the land he had long before promised to Abram. While traveling from

---

[49] 1 Tim 3:15.

[50] 1 Cor 10:11, 2 Tim 3:14–17.

[51] Ecc 1:9; Heb 3:12—4:16.

[52] Gen 12:1–3.

[53] Gen 12–50.

[54] Exod 12:37, 40–41.

Egypt to the Land of Promise, the Israelites received God's Law with the covenant of blessings for obedience and curses for disobedience.

Eventually, the nation of Israel moved to the Promised Land under the leadership of Joshua. After settling the land, the nation endured a time of disobedience, discipline, and deliverance recorded in the book of Judges. The nation then rejected the living God as its King, wanting instead to be like the surrounding nations with a human king.[55]

Part of God's revelation to his people included the standards for what was to happen when they entered the Promised Land and when God set a king over them: the king was to write out for himself a copy of the Law in the presence of the Levitical priests and read it daily so he would learn to fear the Lord and serve God.[56]

When Moses was preparing to transfer leadership to Joshua, he solemnly testified to the people of the importance of paying attention to the covenant of blessings and curses. Moses urged them to obey the words written in the book of the Law.[57] He told them it was not too difficult to obey God's laws and enjoy his covenant blessings.[58] Similarly, Joshua commanded the Israelites to remember the book of the Law and meditate upon it day and night.[59] Joshua called the people to decide for themselves whom they were going to serve—the living God or idols. When they declared their allegiance to the Lord, Joshua again pointed out the importance of obedience and recorded their decision in the book of the Law of God as a witness against them if they forsook their God.[60]

The book of the Law was a safeguard against error and a remedy when error happened. If the people would stick to the book, they would be blessed. If they got off course, they were supposed to return to what the book called them to in the first place. Hold this thought because it is important.

The monarchy was first given to Saul about three hundred years after the death of Joshua. After Saul was rejected as king due to his disobedience

---

[55] 1 Sam 8:7.
[56] Deut 17:14–20.
[57] E.g., Deut 28:1–68, 31:23–30.
[58] Deut 30:10–20.
[59] Josh 1:8.
[60] Josh 24:14–28.

to God, the kingdom was given to David.[61] The united kingdom of Israel endured to the next generation under David's son Solomon. Solomon's downfall was partly a result of disobedience of the people under the leadership of Joshua, when the Israelites failed to properly drive out all the inhabitants of the land in accordance with God's command.[62]

Solomon inherited a situation that was a result of the sins of those who had come before him. He compounded this sin by disobeying God's explicit command to not intermarry with the people of the land (who would not have been there had the Israelites obeyed God's command upon entering the land), which brought forth fruit exactly as God said it would about 450 years later after first settling the Promised Land.[63] As a result, the next generation after Solomon received a divided kingdom; Solomon's son Rehoboam acted foolishly and Israel rebelled, making Jeroboam, the son of Nebat, their king in the north.

Israel was divided into the northern and southern kingdoms, fulfilling God's promise to Solomon in 1 Kings 11:11–13. The northern kingdom went apostate immediately and never turned back, recording not even one king who was considered good in God's sight before it was destroyed under divine discipline by Assyria in 722 BC. The southern kingdom of Judah fared a little better, recording both good and bad kings. It endured a little longer than Israel but was destroyed under divine discipline by Babylon in 586 BC. (For an inspired account of the negative effects the inherited customs of Israel had upon Israel and Judah, read 2 Kings 17:7–23.)

God's people in the kingdom of Judah were eventually taken into exile for seventy years. Afterward, they returned to Jerusalem under the leadership of Zerubbabel, and the walls of the city were rebuilt under the leadership of Nehemiah. The temple was rebuilt under the leadership of Haggai the prophet. The people remained in the land until the close of the Old Testament canon and were still there (albeit under the domain of the Roman Empire) when Jesus was born in fulfillment of the Scriptures.

What's important for us to understand is that each generation inherited

---

[61] 1 Sam 13:13–14. King David was actually the third king of Israel. Saul's son, Ish-bosheth, reigned as king in Israel for two years before David ruled over the united kingdom of Judah and Israel; see 2 Sam 2:8–11; 4:1—5:5.

[62] See Exod 23:23–33, 34:11–17; Deut 7:1–6; 1 Kgs 11:1–13.

[63] Deut 7:3–4.

a culture from the previous generation. Some generations experienced the blessings of obedience, others endured the curses of disobedience, and some experienced both. What is also important for us to recognize is history's cyclical nature. God calls a people to himself, but they wander. God disciplines them according to his Word and brings them back to himself.

Wander, discipline, return. Repeat.

Often, the Lord raises up leaders who institute reforms among the people. When these reforms are in line with God's revealed Word, times of refreshment, renewal, and revival often follow.[64]

When Solomon turned from the living God toward worshiping other gods, he erected places for idol worship.[65] Though some of the kings who followed Solomon did right in God's sight, these "high places" where sacrifices were offered to idols often remained and polluted pure worship of the true and living God. Solomon's son, Rehoboam, the first king of Judah in the divided kingdom, took this idolatry further and built more places of idol worship.

> Judah did evil in the sight of the LORD, and they provoked Him to jealousy more than all that their fathers had done, with the sins which they committed. For they also built for themselves high places and sacred pillars and Asherah poles on every high hill and beneath every luxuriant tree. There were also male cult prostitutes in the land. They did according to all the abominations of the nations which the LORD dispossessed before the sons of Israel. (1 Kgs 14:22–24)

Rehoboam inherited a sinful culture from his father, Solomon, and sank to a new low. Rehoboam's son, Abijam, became king next and walked in his father's sinful ways. As a result of God's favor toward David, God

---

[64] Kaiser, *Revive Us Again* covers sixteen biblical revivals in greater detail than anything presented in the present chapter and is a worthwhile read.

[65] 1 Kgs 11:1–13.

brought about reform in the next generation after Abijam to establish Jerusalem under the good king, Asa.[66]

When Asa became king, he put away the male cult prostitutes, removed all the idols his predecessors had made, removed his mother from being queen because of her idolatrous practices (he cut down the image she had made and burned it), and brought the dedicated things of his father's and his own into the house of the Lord. Asa also commanded Judah to seek the Lord and to obey the Law and Commandments. Despite these reforms, Asa did not take away the high places.[67] Nevertheless, God's inspired Word says that "the heart of Asa was wholly devoted to the LORD all his days."[68] That was a good start.

During the beginning of Asa's reign, the kingdom of Judah was undisturbed by foreign threats while these reforms were taking place because the Lord was giving them rest. Asa took the opportunity to fortify the cities and army of Judah as they sought the Lord in response to the rest God provided. When a threat emerged from Zerah the Ethiopian and his army of 1 million (against the army of 580,000 Judeans), the Lord fought for Judah and routed the Ethiopian army before Asa.[69] Prosperity and peace followed after this victory, all as a result of God's activity among his people after they instituted and walked in reform from what they had inherited from the previous generation.

Kaiser rightly observed,

> In the majority of the revivals in history, it takes tragedy to finally arrest the attention of an apostatizing people of God, but in this case the background for the revival was a reformation. Instead of a time of spiritual famine and religious decline, we are given a surprising exception in the revival under King Asa.[70]

---

[66] 1 Kgs 15:1–7.

[67] 1 Kgs 15:12–15; 2 Chr 14:2–5.

[68] 1 Kgs 15:14b.

[69] 2 Chr 14:5–15.

[70] Kaiser, *Revive Us Again*, 90.

This example is a good place to start because it provides a strong biblical foundation for hope that disaster must not always precede revival.

I know some people who pray for tragedy; they believe only after tragedy strikes that God may revive his people. I am in a different camp. I do not pray for tragedy but for reform because God can likewise use reform to revive his people. If we can be revived without tragedy, that is all for the better. Sadly, it often takes tragedy before we are willing to reform. Sometimes, drastic steps are needed to awaken us from our lethargic state. Biblically aware followers of God should take note of the lengths to which God is willing to go to bring his people back.[71]

Sadly, Asa did not end as well as he began. Despite his failures later in life, his son Jehoshaphat became king in his place and continued in the line of good kings for Judah. He instituted further reforms and followed in the footsteps of his father by ending his reign poorly through a wicked alliance with Ahaziah, the king of Israel.[72] After Jehoshaphat's death, his son Jehoram became king.

Upon taking the throne, Jehoram killed his brothers and began walking in the ways of the apostate kings of Israel, doing evil in the sight of the Lord.[73] Jehoram's wicked reign ended with him dying a painful death under God's curse and with no one regretting his dying.[74] Jehoram's son, Ahaziah, inherited a culture of disobedience and sin and likewise walked in the ways of the apostate kings of Israel. As a result, Ahaziah likewise perished under God's hand.[75]

When Ahaziah was put to death, his mother, Athaliah, took the throne for herself and attempted to kill all Ahaziah's sons who would have had a claim to the throne. Ahaziah's daughter saved one of his sons, Joash, and kept him hidden in the house of God for six years while Athaliah ruled over Judah until the priest Jehoiada was able to put Joash on the throne (leading to the execution of Athaliah).[76]

Despite inheriting an apostate culture, Joash was influenced by the

---

[71] E.g., Amos 4.

[72] 2 Chr 20:35.

[73] 2 Chr 21:1–7.

[74] 2 Chr 21:18–19.

[75] 2 Chr 22:7.

[76] 2 Chr 22:10—23:15.

godly character of Jehoiada the priest, and a covenant was made with the people to seek and serve the Lord—that is, until the godly priest died. After his death, Joash quickly abandoned God and served idols, failing to heed the call of the prophets sent to call the nation back to God. Wrath came upon the kingdom of Judah as a result of Joash's foolishness, and he was succeeded by his son Amaziah, who half-heartedly served the Lord. As had his father, he turned from serving the Lord in his later years.

If the pattern is not evident yet, Amaziah was succeeded by his son Uzziah, who followed in the steps of his father—God prospered him as long as he sought the Lord, but when he turned from God, he was struck with leprosy.[77] Uzziah was succeeded by his son Jotham, who likewise followed in the steps of his father and was blessed as long as he sought the Lord. However, during Jotham's reign, the people of Judah continued to act corruptly.[78]

Jotham's son, Ahaz, succeeded him and led the people back into idolatry. As a result, God's judgment came upon Judah, which led to even further disobedience by Ahaz, leading to Ahaz's closing the temple and making altars for himself in every corner of Jerusalem to burn incense to other gods.

Ahaz's son, Hezekiah, inherited a kingdom saturated in idolatry. Despite this inheritance, Hezekiah opened and repaired the temple and gathered and consecrated the priests. They destroyed the idols, tore down their altars, and reinstituted Passover. One of the idols Hezekiah destroyed was called Nehushtan. Do you know where this idol came from?

When Moses was leading the Israelites in the desert, the people grumbled against the Lord and Moses. In one of these instances, God sent a judgment against his people in the form of fiery serpents to kill the complaining Israelites.[79] When the people cried out for mercy, God provided a means of deliverance that foreshadowed the way God would save his people from their sins through the Messiah.[80] He did so by allowing them to look upon a bronze serpent formed by Moses, which he lifted up on a standard.

---

[77] 2 Chr 26:4–5, 16–21.
[78] 2 Chr 27:2.
[79] Num 21:4–6.
[80] Cf. Num 21:7–9 and John 3:14–15.

After this divine deliverance, they kept the bronze serpent around. Eventually, they began burning incense to it. This object of their deliverance, which was given to magnify the glory and power of the living God, was turned into an object of idolatry and sin when the people worshiped the created thing instead of the Creator. The bronze serpent was named Nehushtan.[81] It was not until nearly seven hundred years later that Hezekiah destroyed this idol. Hundreds of years of idolatry and sin passed from one generation to the next.

If they would have done as God had commanded through Moses and if the kings would have copied and read the Law and obeyed what had been written, the first two of the Ten Commandments could have brought immediate correction and remedy to this disastrous practice. Finally, Hezekiah did what was necessary as he walked with the Lord in obedience to God's revealed will.[82]

As a result of these reforms, God's hand was mightily upon the people and they enjoyed a great time of revival and deliverance from their enemies—even being delivered from Assyria when the northern kingdom of Israel was conquered.[83] This was no small deliverance! Assyria was fierce and greatly to be feared, but God sent an angel to fight for Judah, and the angel killed 185,000 Assyrians. After this massacre, the king of Assyria took his army and returned to Nineveh, where he was killed by his people while worshiping his false god.[84]

This period of great revival under Hezekiah was followed by a new low under his son, Manasseh, who rebuilt all the altars his father had torn down and who worshiped false gods—sacrificing his own sons, practicing sorcery, dealing with mediums and spiritists, and even putting an idol he carved in the temple of God.[85]

Because of Manasseh's great sin and wickedness, God promised to hand Judah over to destruction.[86] Manasseh was succeeded by his son, Amon,

---

[81] 2 Kgs 18:4. Nehushtan shares the same Hebrew root (נחש) as both bronze and serpent.

[82] 2 Kgs 18:5–6.

[83] 2 Kgs 18:7–8.

[84] 2 Kgs 19:32–37.

[85] 2 Chr 33:1–9.

[86] 2 Kgs 23:26; 24:3–4.

who walked in the wicked ways of his father. The cycle of disobedience was once again broken when Amon's son, Josiah, took the throne.

Though we could continue to watch this cyclical nature of God's people, we will end with Josiah. He was very young—only eight—when he became king, but he instituted reforms and sought the Lord, not turning to the right or the left. In the eighteenth year of his reign Josiah ordered repairs to be made to the temple. While the work was being done the book of the Law was discovered.

Upon hearing the reading of the written covenant Josiah tore his clothes. Josiah understood that God's wrath was upon the nation because they had wandered from keeping the covenant and that the book contained the path forward. Josiah gathered all the people, both small and great, and read the book in their presence and the nation recommitted to the covenant. Josiah made reforms in accordance with the book, starting with cleansing the temple and the land of the idolatrous practices they had inherited.[87]

Josiah committed to reforming the nation according to the written Word. "Before him there was no king like him who turned to the LORD with all his heart and with all his soul and with all his might, according to the law of Moses; nor did any like him arise after him" (2 Kgs 23:25). Unfortunately, God's wrath was not able to be turned away because of the great unfaithfulness of Josiah's predecessor, Manasseh.[88]

Do you see how powerful the inheritance can be? In the history of God's people, there are often violent swings between walking with the Lord and walking away from him. We generally see the people following in the footsteps of the leadership. When the kings began wandering from God's Commandments, the people often followed suit. In many cases, the new generation believed whatever it inherited was good and right. Hindsight shows us how terribly wrong many of these inherited practices were and the disastrous fruit of these sinful cultures.

While the particular historical contexts may change—often stemming from some national tragedy or season of despair—one thing seems to remain consistent throughout all these shifts: God is faithful despite his people's unfaithfulness. God calls his people back to himself through

---

[87] 2 Kgs 22:1—23:28.
[88] 2 Kgs 23:26–27.

different means. When God's people hear his Word, reform their practices, and repent from their wandering, God is able and willing to send seasons of revival and rest.

Whether or not God chooses to send revival, the question remains in our day: will we take the time to examine what we have inherited and make the necessary reforms, or will we stubbornly insist that whatever we have inherited is good and right simply because it is what we know? Kaiser rightly stated, "It is not sufficient to know that the Bible is God's Word or to argue for its inerrancy; we must, with a spirit of contriteness and humility, act on the basis of what it says."[89]

I could not agree more. We tend to take our inherited culture for granted. This is especially true of our inherited culture of Christianity. This inheritance shapes the way we view the world and how we interpret the Scriptures. As Christians, we must allow the Scriptures to renew our minds and seek to build our practice on God's revelation instead of conforming ourselves to the patterns of the world, even our "Christian world."[90]

God has given us a glorious gift through his revelation. Each generation must be careful to examine God's Word and its practices. Each generation must reform its ways as necessary to conform to the pattern God has declared.[91] By his grace, we may return and walk in his blessed fellowship and design.

The apostle Peter wrote very near the end of his life,

> This is now, beloved, the second letter I am writing to you in which I am stirring up your sincere mind by way of reminder, that you should remember the words spoken beforehand by the holy prophets and the commandment of the Lord and Savior spoken by your apostles. (2 Pet 3:1–2)

Peter referred to his first letter, 1 Peter, which had been addressed to different regions where Paul had planted churches throughout the Greco-Roman

---

[89] Kaiser, *Revive Us Again*, 143.

[90] Rom 12:2; Jas 1:22–27; Matt 7:24–27.

[91] For an extended discussion on the need for revision and reform, see Viola, *Revise Us Again*.

empire. The apostle urged them to remember the words spoken beforehand by the holy prophets and the commandment of the Lord and Savior spoken by the apostles. Peter was appealing to the foundation of the apostles and prophets being the basis for a healthy church culture.

We must not mistakenly think our church culture is healthy simply because our fellowship is growing in number or because we haven't endured some terrible scandal. Instead, we must judge the health of our church culture by examining how firmly it is built upon the apostolic foundation as revealed in the Scriptures. With that in mind, we turn our attention to the church in the next chapter.

CHAPTER 3

The Church

Now to Him who is able to do far more abundantly beyond all that we ask or think, according to the power that works within us, to Him be the glory in the church and in Christ Jesus to all generations forever and ever. Amen.
—Ephesians 3:20–21

Those looking for a detailed theology of the church can find many excellent resources;[92] I will not attempt to reproduce the solid work that has been done elsewhere. Instead, in this chapter, I will outline in broad strokes what the church is and for whom it exists. After this framework is outlined, the following chapter will examine the practice of the apostle Paul in his church-planting ministry, a study often neglected in theological discussions of the church and treated as its own division of Pauline studies.[93] This is a shame. Paul's foundational work as an apostle in building the church should not be separated from our theological understanding of the church itself.[94] It is only when we build on the genuine apostolic foundation that we will rightly understand Christ's church. Our theory always affects our practice.

So what is the church? This is one of those areas in which our language can lead us astray. Popular use of the word *church* contributes to misconceptions. Though I know the building where we hold worship

---

[92] A good place to start is Geisler, *Systematic Theology*, 4:17–244; Grudem, *Systematic Theology*, 851–1088; Erickson, *Christian Theology*, 1033–1152; and Viola, *Reimagining Church*.

[93] An exception to this is Viola, *The Untold Story of the New Testament Church*.

[94] Eph 2:11—3:10.

services is not the church, I still find myself saying, "I'll meet you at the church." "I'm headed to the church." "The church needs a new roof." But the building is not the church, and the people I speak that way with know that, but unfortunately, not everyone does. Many who are not a part of the church think the church is the building. Many who profess to be a part of the church do so on the basis of their sitting in church regularly, even if "regularly" turns out to be only once a decade. Some people even think God lives in the building and we go there to visit him Sunday mornings. I once filed a book for my children that taught this very thing in its appropriate place, the garbage.

The language we use is powerful. Even when we understand the church is not the building, we can still fall into patterns of behavior that have been influenced by this idea. Some people rightly understand the church building is not the church but wrongly conclude it is the place for church ministry. They view it the way they would a hospital or a department store where doctors or merchants are hard at work. While some doctors make house calls, they are not random house calls, and merchants usually do their selling at their stores, not house to house. In the same way, some believe Christianity is rightly confined to buildings constructed for those purposes. Extenuating circumstances aside, the building is the appropriate venue for all things Christian.

While proclaiming the gospel in public places, I meet many professing Christians and non-Christians who hold this view. Usually, those who get the angriest with my trying to talk about Jesus with them are those who have already "gone to church" that week. They view my conversation with them as inappropriate because it is not being confined to the appropriate place, the church building. I once offered to give a gentleman who raised such an objection a ride to a church so we could continue the conversation there. He declined.

Regardless of some of these popular misconceptions, the church existed long before the first church building was ever built.[95] The Scriptures describe God's church as a building of a different sort: a building composed of people, not for people. The people are the building.

In 1 Corinthians 6, the apostle Paul addressed believers who had immorality in their midst.

---

[95] For more, see Viola and Barna, *Pagan Christianity?* chapter 2.

> Or do you not know that your body is a temple of the
> Holy Spirit who is in you, whom you have from God,
> and that you are not your own? For you have been bought
> with a price: therefore glorify God in your body. (1 Cor
> 6:19–20)

Paul's use of pronouns and verbs is very helpful in demonstrating the point. It is easy to miss in English translations, but in the original Greek, the "you" he used repeatedly was plural while the "body" was singular, and his verbs corresponded to this reality. Paul did not write, "Or do you (plural) not know (plural) that your *bodies* (plural) *are* (plural) temples (plural) of the Holy Spirit."[96] This is significant. Instead, he wrote your (plural) body (singular) is (singular) a temple (singular) for the Holy Spirit who is in you (plural), therefore glorify (plural) God in your body (singular). Paul understood that the "church building" the Holy Spirit lived in was the collective people of God; the church was the people; the people were the building.[97]

This is not a denial of the presence of God in individuals. We can affirm the reality of the indwelling Spirit in all born-again Christians individually and affirm the Holy Spirit also dwells in the entire body at the same time;[98] these truths are not mutually exclusive. The point of the present discussion is that I am not the church and neither are you; we are the church, the body of Christ, the bride of Christ together and collectively.

As a result of this theological understanding, the apostle was asserting that sin in one person affected others.[99] This transcends whatever building we may congregate in whether a home or a stadium and extends to when we are not in any building.

In this sense, we can affirm that the church is indeed where Christian

---

[96] The TNIV renders the text as "Do you not know that your bodies are temples of the Holy Spirit," making "bodies," "temples," and the verb "to be" plural when the Greek text has them as singular. This is a mistake in my judgment, and a more accurate translation is found in the HSCB, ESV, KJV, NAB, NASB, NET, NIV, NKJV, NLT, and NRSV, which all preserve the singular form of body and temple, though the form of "you" in English is ambiguous.

[97] See also 1 Pet 2:4–11.

[98] 1 Cor 12:12–27.

[99] 1 Cor 12:26.

ministry happens. We also need to understand and affirm that this means ministry happens wherever Christians are. If we are followers of Christ, the church exists wherever we are. This is why theologians refer to the church gathered and the church scattered. When we gather, something special happens. However, the church is not a location but the collective people of God comprising Jew and Gentile who are in Christ.

A related principle is taught regarding marriage. When a man and woman come together as husband and wife, they are spiritually joined and become one flesh.[100] This spiritual union transcends space and time; my wife and I are still married even when she is at the grocery store and I am at work. In the same way, as members of the church, we are God's people when we are together and when we are separated.

When we allow the false idea of the church being a place rather than the people of God, we invite many harmful consequences. For one, we redefine the scope of where our light is allowed to shine by confining it to structures built for that purpose. Perhaps even more problematic is that we begin to define our unity based on those who gather with us in a particular location. This was happening in Corinth, and Paul rebuked it sharply.[101] When we misunderstand what the church is and allow our language and culture to reshape and redefine it, we begin to lose sight of whom the church is for. If taken too far, this can result in the church living for our misconstrued purposes instead of for the purposes God called us to.

The full answer to the question of whom the church is for is nuanced. The church is for God, for believers, and for the world, but it is not for each of these in the same way. First, the church is for God. Paul wrote that his particular ministry was

> to bring to light what is the administration of the mystery which for ages has been hidden in God who created all things; so that the manifold wisdom of God might now be made known through the church to the rulers and the authorities in the heavenly places. This was in accordance with the eternal purpose which He carried out in Christ Jesus our Lord. (Eph 3:9–11)

---

[100] Gen 2:24.

[101] 1 Cor 1:10–13. For more on this see, Kohler, *Gate Crashers*, 122–47.

Through the church, God is making known his wisdom to the rulers and authorities in heavenly places. The glory and purpose of the church extends beyond simply what we can know, experience, and describe. God's mission of redeeming a people for himself from every tribe, tongue, and nation from under the curse upon them for rebellion against God is being accomplished through Christ. Jesus has fulfilled his earthly ministry as Savior in fulfillment of the Scriptures, has been exalted to the right hand of the Father, and is working through the church on earth to complete the task of gathering a people for himself to present the people of God to the Father on the day of Christ Jesus.[102] These redeemed people's purpose is to exalt the glorious grace of God[103] and demonstrate his mercy in contrast to the enemies, which he will put under his feet.[104] This is the eternal purpose of God in Christ.

When the church walks in accordance with God's plan (revealed through the apostle Paul's letter to the saints in Ephesus) as the fullness of Christ on earth, the redeemed of God—the church—are in stark contrast to those who will perish in their sins under God's righteous wrath. For this contrast to be a reality there must be a clear differentiation between the church and the world. This contrast is blurred when we buy into the modern ideas of blending in with the world to be relevant.[105]

The church exists (at least partially) for demonstrating God's glorious grace and mercy given through Christ and for demonstrating God's sovereignty over every kingdom on earth by redeeming people from every tribe, tongue, and nation. God's purpose is for his church to make his excellencies and glory known to all creation and to magnify his compassion, mercy, and grace.[106]

---

[102] 1 Cor 15:22–24.

[103] Eph 1:3–14.

[104] Rom 9:23–26; 16:20; 1 Cor 15:25–26.

[105] See chapter 1. This same contrasting purpose of the church and the world is expressed by Paul in Rom 9:13–26. This is one reason why salvation cannot in any way be based upon the merit or works of the individual who is saved, but must be evidence of God's grace in the lives of the redeemed (Eph 2:8–9; Titus 3:4–7). Otherwise, salvation would not be an example of grace and mercy.

[106] E.g., Luke 4:43; John 12:27–28; Acts 20:17–27, 26:16–18; Rom 8:28—11:36; 2 Cor 5:1–21; Eph 1:9–14, 3:8–13.

Sadly, it is possible to reject God's purpose.[107] This is why followers of Christ are encouraged to be unified with each other in accordance with God's purpose.[108] Understanding God's purpose for his church gives us direction for our gatherings and for when we are dispersed.

The first of these (the church gathered) addresses how the church is for believers. The second (the church dispersed) addresses how the church is for the world. When believers gather, they do so to worship God as a body and to edify each other through prayer, the exercise of their spiritual gifts, singing, tithing, participating in the ordinances of baptism and communion, and being instructed through the Word of God preached and taught.

When the church disperses from the corporate gathering, believers worship God as a body through the evangelization of the world by the bold, faithful, and loving proclamation of the gospel of the kingdom of God and by living as children of light in the midst of a dark world, demonstrating their love through service and works of mercy, compassion, and justice.

In our culture, these differing purposes are often mingled. Some strands of theology relating to the church have actually attempted to invite as many nonbelievers (the unchurched) as possible into the corporate gatherings to expose them to the gospel. Our contemporary usage of the word *church* makes it possible to say some unregenerate people are members of the church simply because they regularly participate in the services and have taken the steps necessary to achieve membership in the visible organization.

When we shift our focus from conversion to assimilation, we begin to emphasize attendance and membership over the new birth and new life in Christ. Modern evangelism methods can reduce conversion to a decision made with every head bowed and every eye closed. People repeat a prayer and judge their own sincerity. This makes the biblical emphasis of making our calling and election sure by examining the fruit of our own professions

---

[107] Luke 7:24–35.

[108] Phil 2:1–13; Col 1:25–29; 1 Thess 4:1–7; 2 Tim 1:8–14, 3:9–15; 1 Pet 2:1–25, 4:1–11.

of faith and the fruit of the professions of our brothers and sisters in Christ legalistic and judgmental.[109]

We are not the first generation of Christians to wrestle with these issues. Historian Earl Cairns wrote of the church in the so-called Dark Ages hastily incorporating as many as possible into the fellowship of the visible organization and accommodating church practices to make the masses more comfortable by establishing new traditions and patterns reminiscent of their previous ways of life. Cairns stated that after evangelizing the barbarians who were coming into the Roman Empire,

> many of them brought old patterns of life and customs with them into the church. Saint worship was substituted for the old hero worship. Many ritualistic practices that savored of paganism found an open door into the church. The church, in attempting to meet the need of the barbarians, was itself partially paganized.[110]

While many (especially Protestants) realize the error in saint worship, we are not immune from making similar accommodations and concessions today. My evangelist, Joel Davidson, recalls being part of a meeting regarding music selection in the church when a longtime member of a local church suggested they stop singing songs about the blood of Christ because their neighbors and friends who visited felt uncomfortable singing about such things. The heart of the suggestion was to make "church" comfortable for nonbelievers so they would keep attending—as if sitting in church once a week were the goal of bringing people to Christ.

Regardless of our human terminology, the genuine church comprises only those who have been born again by the Spirit of God. Any attempt to gather as many unregenerate people as possible is not rightfully called a church service; it is probably better called an evangelistic outreach.

Some argue that attempts to gather as many people who are not followers of Christ and confront them with the truth of the gospel message is a reasonable activity, but such a discussion extends beyond the purposes of this chapter, which is about the wisdom of calling such mingled gatherings

---

[109] E.g., 2 Pet 1:10–11; Phil 2:12; 1 Cor 5:1–13; 2 Cor 13:5.
[110] Cairns, *Christianity Throughout the Centuries*, 124.

of believers and nonbelievers church. I affirm what Norman Geisler stated regarding the reality of nonbelievers being a part of the corporate worship services in Corinth.

> Further, Paul refers to unbelievers coming into the local church and being convinced by the message (1 Cor. 14:24). The service was not primarily for evangelism of unbelievers, but for edification of believers; nonetheless, *edification is the internal mission of the church, and evangelism is the external mission.*[111]

To be as faithful as we can to biblical revelation, we shouldn't mingle the purposes of the church gathered and the church scattered. When we mingle these differing purposes, we dilute them to the detriment of both. We sure shouldn't prohibit nonbelievers from entering the assembly, but when we cater to nonbelievers, we must recognize we are altering the purpose of the gathering according to God's design. Edification of believers gets sacrificed on the altar of evangelization of and entertaining the lost. Consequently, evangelization of the lost is actually hindered because the body does not participate fully in the command to make disciples but wrongfully delegates the task (most often to the pastor), thinking it is their duty to merely invite nonbelievers to their church services and events. Wayne Grudem agreed with this idea.

> Though Scripture does not emphasize evangelism as a primary purpose when the church meets for worship, Paul does tell the Corinthians to take thought for unbelievers and outsiders who come to their services, to be sure that the Christians speak in understandable ways (see 1 Cor. 14:23). ... But evangelism is not seen as a primary purpose when the church assembles for worship, and it would therefore not be right to have the only weekly gathering of believers designed primarily with an evangelistic purpose.[112]

---

[111] Geisler, *Systematic Theology*, 4:95; italics in original.
[112] Grudem, *Systematic Theology*, 1009.

The primary purpose of the Christian gathering is not the evangelization of nonbelievers but the edification of believers and the worship of God by and with the assembled family of God.

Speaking in understandable ways, not in complicated religious jargon, is important so unbelievers who enter the assembly will understand why we are doing what we're doing—including the strange activities of singing about the blood of Jesus and proclaiming salvation through repentance and faith in the risen Christ alone.

This is not to undermine the importance of evangelism; quite the contrary. What these "seeker-sensitive" models have done, most likely by accident, is hinder the evangelization of the world because edification of believers is not emphasized to the proper degree. It is often argued that with such a model, we cannot go too deep because we will not be relevant to the nonbeliever. Such sentiment sounds good, but it is contrary to the apostle Paul's counsel. For Paul, a "relevant" church service is one in which the Spirit of God is moving—making it hard to have a series of identical services that are all exactly one hour long—and in which unbelievers will enter, be convicted of their sin, and realize God is present in the assembly.[113] The apostolic admonition was not to keep sermons to a minimum and entertainment to the maximum, to quench the exercise of spiritual gifts, or to minimize discussions of sin. Instead, Paul urged the use of spiritual gifts, to allow more than one preacher time to preach, and to do all things for the purpose of edification!

Properly edified and equipped believers will be much more effective in evangelizing their unsaved friends, families, neighbors, and acquaintances because they will live their lives for that purpose instead of relying on special events and one-hour worship services once a week to accomplish it. Non-Christian coworkers may never attend church potlucks, but they will be exposed to their Christian coworkers forty hours a week!

It is only when the entire body is edified and mature that the third and final purpose of the church can be properly fulfilled. The risen Jesus gave leadership to the saints for ministry, not to be the sole doers of ministry.[114] The primary purpose of the church assembled is for edification;

---

[113] 1 Cor 14:23–33.

[114] There is a fair amount of debate on the role of leadership in equipping the saints and to the proper interpretation of Ephesians 4:11–12. T. David Gordon

an edified, mature body can fulfill the purpose of the church in and toward the world—evangelism.[115] Edification (the church gathered) and evangelization (the church scattered) are activities of a people who live in worship of their God and Savior.

Some may object to the dichotomy and point to the command to make disciples (which is more than a call to simply evangelize). However, understanding the different focuses of the church assembled and the church scattered encompasses the call to make disciples. As the church scatters and proclaims Christ, those who respond with repentance and faith are initiated into the family of God through baptism, and then they are incorporated into the church for the purpose of edification. As each individual member of the church is built up, he or she participates in the major activities of the church assembled and scattered. When believers encounter the needs of the world and the needs of the body, they will address those needs in practical ways.[116] This is how disciples are made; they become part of the life of the body and function in accordance with God's eternal purposes.

Millard Erickson accurately observed that "the second major function of the church is the edification of believers. Though Jesus laid greater emphasis on evangelism, the edification of believers is logically prior."[117] When we mingle the priorities of the church and alter our services to cater to the evangelism and entertainment of the nonbeliever instead of

---

argued in his article "'Equipping' Ministry In Ephesians 4?" that the KJV had properly punctuated Ephesians 4:12 and that it was wrong to reduce the function of leadership in the church to simply the equipping of the saints. To reduce the ministry of leadership to simply equipping the saints is almost certainly incorrect, but the reality of equipping the saints cannot be rejected as at least part of the ministry of leadership. The syntax of Ephesians 4:12 is too complex to resolve here, because as Dunn rightly identified, "commentators are almost equally divided on the point" (Dunn, *Theology of Paul*, 5/4n42).

[115] Works of service, mercy, and justice fall into the category of evangelism when they are done in conjunction with verbally sharing the gospel message. To do works of service, mercy, and justice without including the gospel is to minister to temporary needs while neglecting the more serious, eternal need of salvation. When we do both, we are walking in the design of our living God. See also Lindsell, "Biblical Basis of Missions," 149–50.

[116] E.g., Matt 25:31–46; Jas 1:27, 2:14–26; Gal 6:10; Titus 3:1, 8, 14.

[117] Erickson, *Christian Theology*, 1063.

the edification of the believer, we do a disservice to both. When we fail to properly equip and edify the body, the work of evangelism becomes restricted to a few "professionals." It is likewise restricted to a small sector of time and geography by being constrained to our services designed for such purposes. When this happens, none of the actual purposes of God are met fully. God did not design his church to proclaim his glory for one hour on Sunday mornings before football starts.

Such deviations from God's design may seem subtle, but the consequences run deep. When we compare the power and impact of the early church with the contemporary church, we see the differences more starkly. Are you not alarmed by the differences between the church recorded in Acts and the earliest centuries and our contemporary experience? In our present culture, we have churches on every corner, yet according to some sources, America has the third-largest population of unreached people groups in the world.[118]

How can so many churches be having such a minimal impact in the spreading of the gospel throughout our land? The answer is because we have drifted from God's revealed purposes and designs for the edification of his church into full maturity and the stature that belongs to the fullness of Christ as outlined in Ephesians 4:11–16.

We have become very good at running the church like a business and building our mini-kingdoms of denominationalism. We have excelled at using modern methods and media to entertain the masses. However, we have done a bad job of glorifying God through declaring his gospel to the ends of the earth. We are doing a bad job at this currently, at least partially, because we are not building our theology of church on the right leadership foundation. Instead of a biblical model, we are building on a model inherited from church structures that had been greatly influenced by pagan practices.[119] Our attempts to modify God's design have decreased our ability to edify and equip the body. This hinders the task of world

---

[118] Payne, *Unreached Peoples*. E-book available from www.jdpayne.org/wp-content/uploads/2014/02/Unreached-Peoples-Least-Reached-Places-Payne.pdf. Accessed November 18, 2015.

[119] For a more detailed discussion of this, see Viola and Barna, *Pagan Christianity?* chapter 5.

evangelization because many members of the body are still infants, being tossed to and fro by every new doctrine.[120]

The churches Paul planted were different in their potency. Some think they were more effective because the culture was more accommodating and accepting of the gospel message, but this is inaccurate.[121] Instead, their potency came from the fact they did not drift as far from the foundation as we have. When they began to drift, the apostles were still alive and brought them back to greater conformity to God's revealed will and design. Though the apostles are no longer living in the flesh, we thankfully retain their inspired correction and encouragement in the New Testament.

As we examine Paul's church-planting practice, will we be willing to reform our practices and church structures to be faithful to what God has intended if we have strayed from his design?

Brian—A Testimony

(Brian is a staff/clinical pharmacist who personally shares the gospel with hundreds of individuals per year.)

I grew up in the church, but when I was in high school, I was doing things all the other kids were doing, and this got worse in college when I lived in my own apartment and there were no parents around to curtail my freedom to walk in the lusts of my flesh.

During college, I met Brenda, whom I later married. After graduation in 2006, she moved back to my hometown as we planned on getting married soon after college. I believed myself to be saved at that time, and my uncle Todd, a pastor, married us in the spring of 2007.

During the first year or so of matrimony, things became horrible largely because my life had been a sham and a lie. I had lied to Brenda about so many things, mainly my wandering eyes and heart leading up to our wedding, not to mention the filthy images I would stare at on the Internet and the TV when she was gone or asleep.

At the time, we were attending the church I'd grown up in. Our

---

[120] Eph 4:12–16.

[121] For a good overview of the advantages they had and the challenges the early church faced, see Green, *Evangelism Now & Then*, 16–21.

church offered "The Way of the Master," a class by Ray Comfort and Kirk Cameron, and we began going through the teaching series.[122] I sat through a couple of those videos hoping to learn how to share my faith.

One day, I was reading through the Commandments; all I really remember is that the commandment "Thou shalt not lie" was impressed upon my heart and I was unable to escape it. I admitted I was either a backslidden hypocrite or was not actually saved at all, neither of which I was comfortable with. I knew I would have to come clean with Brenda about my lying in the past four to five years of our relationship.

On June 26, 2009, I finally brought myself to talk to Brenda about all this. You know it's bad when you begin a conversation with, "You'll probably want to divorce me for what I'm about to tell you." Praise God, Brenda and I are still married today and much more happily now. But on that day, a shouting match ensued and continued for about an hour until Brenda left for work. I sat on the steps outside our living room and cried out to God, "Lord, I don't even know if I am saved, but if I'm not, I want to be!" I believe I was genuinely saved that day. Either that or I was chastened and brought back into the fold; I am not sure exactly which. But I know now that by God's grace I'll never go back to the place I had been.

The weeks and months after that conversation were the hardest of my life. I was, however, reading my Bible at a pace I'd never read it in the past. I read the New Testament in just a matter of weeks. It took a year, maybe two, for things to get back to some semblance of normal between Brenda and me.

The next spring, we visited Chuck—one of my old college roommates who lived in Arizona. We met my other roommate, Dusty, and his wife, Sarah, there as well. While making the three-hour drive from Chuck's house to visit the Grand Canyon, Dusty, Sarah, Brenda, and I, all of whom are pharmacists, talked about birth control. I told the group I was becoming convinced that as Christians, we shouldn't be using them due to their potential abortifacient effects even if this effect occurred only a small percentage of the time. A couple months later, Brenda and I decided we'd no longer use this method for our family. In December 2010, Brenda gave birth to our first son, Ezra.

From 2010 to 2012, our church had an outreach booth (it still does) at

---

[122] You can learn more about The Way of the Master at www.wayofthemaster.com.

the county fair to give away calendars with the gospel message on the back. We would take a picture of the people and their families, print them on a calendar, laminate them, and talk to them about the gospel when it was time to give them the calendar. I came to enjoy this activity very much. Growing up in church, I had learned lots of things I had never put into practice. At that point, I was actually obeying the Lord and walking in the light of what he revealed.

We did this outreach each year during fair week, and I looked forward to it each summer. I asked my pastor why we didn't do this at other festivals and more times per year. His response was basically that it was hard to organize and get people interested in going. I didn't understand that as it seemed the people I was ministering with seemed excited to be there.

Brenda and I were working as pharmacists in the retail setting and dispensing oral contraceptives regularly. After a while, it began to eat at me. I knew it wasn't right for me to use these drugs personally, and I wasn't sure what my culpability was in the whole process as someone who sold them. I wanted to do my job, but I didn't want to be responsible for the death of a conceived child even if I were just the middle man. I read "Does the Birth Control Pill Cause Abortions?" by Randy Alcorn[123] and it confirmed what I had been feeling. I was convinced that I couldn't and wouldn't dispense these "medications" anymore. I tried to work something out with my employer at that time but to no avail. It became overwhelmingly evident that I'd have to change my career to get away from this practice so I could live with myself.

In April 2012, I applied for a residency position so I could gain experience in hospital pharmacy. Of the three hospitals I applied to, I only received one interview. This made my part easy; I only had one location on my list. Thankfully, I matched with that hospital and landed the position as a postgraduate year-one resident, which was comical considering I'd been out of school for about six years then.

During that year, my income was about a third of what it had been at the retail pharmacy, and my commute increased from sixteen minutes to fifty minutes each way. But as the Lord would have it, I would redeem the

---

[123] This free e-book is available online at www.epm.org/static/uploads/downloads/ bcpill.pdf.

time listening to Todd Friel on Wretched Radio[124] and to my uncle Todd's sermons. During this time, I developed even more of a desire to evangelize. I tried to evangelize a few people at work and began doing so even more so as my time at my first job was ending, knowing the opportunity to share with my colleagues was coming to an end.

After the residency ended, I found a job at a hospital in Howell, MI. I was driving an hour and fifteen minutes one way for the first two months. Though I enjoyed listening to Mr. Friel during those trips, I knew we'd need to move closer and soon since I was growing weary of the daily commute. We closed on the purchase of our new home in Howell, an eight-minute drive from the hospital, at the end of August 2013. Being new to the area, we needed to find a new church home. We began by looking at churches on the Internet for places that were close and that at least on first appearance were solid biblically.

Prior to October 2013, I had never been to a church that had an evangelist on staff or as part of the leadership team. We visited several churches during those first few months. We visited traditional denominational churches as well as hip, seeker-friendly churches, and a few in between.

At one of the in-between churches, I met Aaron Hathaway, the evangelist at the church we were visiting the next town over. We had gone to that church a few times, and we started to become familiar with the faces at this new place. Aaron was a friendly face and about our age, so we decided to ask him and his family over to watch the Super Bowl. As it turned out, none of us really cared about the game, but we used it as an excuse to get to know one another. The game was a blowout, and since we were trying to avoid the oftentimes racy commercials, Aaron and I talked in my office for about two hours about theology and the Bible. It seemed that Aaron and I were on the same page with everything we talked about. I was excited he was in a leadership position at the new church we had been attending.

Several weeks later, because Aaron was the evangelist, he asked me if I would like to come witnessing with a group of guys after church. I was excited to do that. I had wanted to get out and do that regularly, but I had

---

[124] www.wretchedradio.com.

found I wasn't brave enough to hit the streets on my own; I was used to being in a group when we'd ministered at the fair.

Aaron was a little surprised when I actually got into his car to meet some guys downtown to witness. He said that people often told him "I would love to go out witnessing sometime" but that I was one of the few who actually took him up on it right away.

He and I walked around downtown together, and I was able to use much of the training I received from Way of the Master and Wretched Radio as we passed out tracts and tried to get into conversations with people. That Sunday, I met Pastor Joe Kohler and Joel Davidson who, as it turns out, was an evangelist as well.

This brings us to the present. Our family—Brenda, Ezra, Elisha, and I—now attend a fellowship that was planted in our new hometown. It started in Aaron's living room, moved to Pastor Joe's basement, and ended up in an old but converted barn we meet in now. Despite our small and humble meeting place, the Lord has used a small group of men and their families to sow many thousands of gospel seeds in Livingston County and Southeast Michigan.

I have seen firsthand what "church" looks like most of my life. I have attended places where there was no recognized evangelist, places where there was a recognized evangelist but no unity about the function and authority of the office, and now a place where the evangelist is recognized and emphasized as an important part of the leadership structure.

Prior to the in-between church, I had never heard of an evangelist position at a church. I thought of evangelists as people who went around speaking at special events or special church gatherings. It was the first time I had been asked to go out to evangelize on an ordinary Sunday during which there were no special functions going on such as the fair ministries I'd been involved in. I thought the church I grew up in had been one of the most evangelistically minded churches around. Now that I am attending a body where there is an evangelist who is part of the leadership structure, I can see a major difference in the frequency that the gospel is shared outside the walls of the building.

I also now see how the pastor can thrive in his role of teaching and shepherding while the evangelist is leading the congregation to bring the good news to the lost. One time, a man from the church's neighborhood talked with Pastor Joe right after a Sunday morning service. We were just about to go out witnessing. I told Evangelist Joel I wanted to wait for Pastor Joe and would catch up with the rest of the group in a little while. Joel reminded me that Pastor Joe might be ministering to that person for an hour or even longer and that I should just come with him and the others.

Sure enough, once we got back from passing out tracts and witnessing, Pastor Joe's and the man's cars were still in the parking lot. Had I stayed behind, I wouldn't have been able to go out with the group and fewer people would have received a tract, or Pastor Joe might have been hurried or inhibited from ministering to the man who had wandered in.

Having an evangelist who makes plans to hit the streets with others has been helpful in keeping us on task and busy in the work of the Lord. My son Ezra knows that every week after our church service, daddy will be out witnessing with "the guys." Being obedient to the Lord and fulfilling the Great Commission isn't nearly as intimidating when a group is doing so in unity and in love for each other as the body of Christ.

I am so grateful for Aaron's invitation to witness together. The Lord used it to lead our family to our church and to a deep bond and brotherly love that has developed from ministering with "the guys."

CHAPTER 4

Paul's Churches

For the word of the Lord has sounded forth from you, not only in Macedonia and Achaia, but also in every place your faith toward God has gone forth, so that we have no need to say anything.
—1 Thessalonians 1:8

It would be hard to overemphasize Paul's fame as an apostle and his importance to the Christian faith. I marvel at the distance he traveled to spread the gospel to the ends of the Roman Empire. When you study Paul's church-planting journeys, you will be astonished at how much ground he covered. We have the good fortune of being able to look back at his practices to see how he was able to be used so fruitfully for the Lord.

When many people think of Paul, they think of him as a missionary, but it is more accurate to think of him as a church planter.[125] Many commentators and Bible headings have used the terminology of "Paul's missionary journeys" (first missionary journey, second, etc.), but that is a bit misleading.

Immediately after Paul's conversion, he remained with the disciples in Damascus and began proclaiming Jesus as the Son of God in the synagogues, going to Arabia and returning to Damascus.[126] This bold

---

[125] I thank my ministry partner, Joel Davidson, for bringing much of Paul's church-planting efforts to the focus in our church family. The result of his study and teaching in this area has greatly enriched my own understanding, and I am grateful for his in-depth study of this in shaping the material in this chapter and driving me to study this topic in greater depth.

[126] Gal 2:13–18; Acts 9:1–26.

proclamation resulted in opposition from the Jews he was refuting in Damascus, and he fled to Jerusalem due to a plan to kill him. His reputation as an opponent of Christianity made it difficult for him to associate with the believers in Jerusalem until Barnabas endorsed Paul's ministry to the apostles. After this, Paul freely preached Christ in Jerusalem until the Hellenistic Jews there decided to put him to death. Once again, Paul fled, this time to Caesarea and to Tarsus, his hometown.

After Stephen was martyred, a great persecution began in Jerusalem that drove all the believers (except the apostles) into the surrounding areas.[127] Some of these scattered believers found their way to Antioch, where they preached to Jews and Gentiles. After hearing about the favor of the Lord being expressed in Antioch, the apostles sent Barnabas to check it out. Barnabas observed the grace of God being poured out in Antioch and then traveled to Tarsus to look for Paul. He brought Paul back with him to Antioch, where Paul and Barnabas stayed for a year and taught there.[128] This all happened prior to the so-called first missionary journey.

On Paul's first church-planting journey (c. AD 46–48), Paul left from his sending church in Antioch with Barnabas. They traveled down to the port city of Seleucia and sailed to Cyprus, where they preached the Word of God in the synagogues of Salamis. After traveling through the entire island as far as Paphos, they set sail and came to Perga in Pamphylia, and from there, they traveled to Pisidian Antioch,[129] where they proclaimed the Word of God in the synagogue. When the Jews rejected the gospel message, Paul and Barnabas turned their attention to the Gentiles. The Word of God was being spread through the region.

As a result of the spread of the Word of God, the Jews instigated a persecution against Paul and Barnabas. They stirred up prominent women and leading men of the city, who drove Paul and Barnabas out of the region. So Paul and Barnabas traveled to Iconium, where they led many—Jew and Gentile alike—to faith in Christ by speaking the Word in the synagogue.

Again, the Jews began stirring up dissension and opposition to the message of Paul and the city became divided. In Iconium, Jews and Gentiles tried to stone him and Barnabas to death. They became aware

---

[127] Acts 8:1. Note that Saul was the leader of this persecution prior to his conversion.
[128] Acts 11:19–27.
[129] Not to be confused with Syrian Antioch, where they set out from.

of this plot and fled to the cities of Lycaonia, Lystra, and Derbe and the surrounding region and continued to proclaim the gospel there.

Paul's opponents were not content simply to have him leave; they wanted him dead. They followed him from Pisidian Antioch and Iconium and won over the crowds against Paul in Lystra; they stoned him and dragged him out of the city. There is some ambiguity in the text, but stoning was a punishment to death, and at the very least, Paul's opponents thought he was dead. But Paul revived in miraculous fashion after the disciples stood around him, and he continued on his way. Whether Paul actually died and was resuscitated is a matter of speculation.[130] The next day, Paul left with Barnabas for Derbe, where they preached the gospel and made many disciples. All this missionary activity is described in Acts 13:1–14:21.

Up until this point, we have seen great evangelistic zeal and effectiveness in bringing the gospel to new places and peoples. However, what happened next was incredibly important for us in rightly understanding Paul's foundational ministry.

From Derbe, Paul could have traveled back through his hometown of Tarsus and back to his sending church in Antioch. That was a direct route home and would have been a natural way to conclude a missionary journey. Paul and Barnabas had experienced much fruit and had a good deal to report, which they did.[131] Instead of this, however, we get a few short verses that are easily skimmed over.

> After they had preached the gospel to that city [Derbe] and had made many disciples, they returned to Lystra and to Iconium and to Antioch, strengthening the souls of the disciples, encouraging them to continue in the faith, and saying, "Through many tribulations we must enter the kingdom of God." When they had appointed elders for them in every church, having prayed with fasting, they commended them to the Lord in whom they had believed. They passed through Pisidia and came into Pamphylia. When they had spoken the word in Perga, they went down to Attalia. (Acts 14:21–25)

---

[130] Acts 14:19–20.
[131] Acts 14:26–27.

Paul and Barnabas did not simply travel to an area and preach the gospel. After traveling from the region of Pamphylia, they went to Pisidian Antioch,[132] to Iconium, to Lystra, and finally to Derbe. Though persecution kept on pushing them out of these places, they returned to strengthen the churches and establish leadership in the form of elders in every church. Only after returning to strengthen the churches did they return to their sending church in Antioch and report on all the things God had done with them. After returning home, Paul and Barnabas spent a long time with the disciples in Antioch.[133]

Paul understood the importance of bold, faithful, and loving proclamation of the gospel, but he did not stop there. He also recognized the importance of communities of believers being faithfully established, equipped, and edified. As a result of this understanding of his role in building a foundation for the church, Paul did not simply evangelize and leave the rest to the Holy Spirit.

Instead, as Paul walked with the Holy Spirit, he proclaimed the gospel and established churches with sustainable leadership; he dedicated himself to long periods of fellowship, teaching, and the edification of believers. Paul was not focused just on evangelizing the world by himself as a missionary but also on building up the church. He knew the body of Christ could do far more than any one member of the body could.

Paul remained in Antioch until a disturbance arose over the relationship between Jews and Gentiles in the church. Some men came from Judea to Antioch and were teaching that circumcision was necessary for salvation. This teaching caused great dissension, and eventually, the church at Antioch decided to send Paul, Barnabas, and some others to the elders and apostles in Jerusalem to settle the matter. The result of this conference[134] was the theological understanding that the Gentiles were not to be compelled to be circumcised or keep the Law of Moses to earn salvation. Salvation was

---

[132] This is the Antioch referred to in Acts 14:21, not to be confused with Paul's sending church, which was in Syrian Antioch.

[133] Acts 14:26–28.

[134] Typical language calls this the Jerusalem council, but I am inclined to agree with Geisler, who pointed out that only two churches were directly involved—Antioch and Jerusalem—and since delegates from all the other churches were not involved, this is not really a true "council" (Geisler, *Systematic Theology*, 4:71).

the gift of God by grace through faith for Jew and Gentile alike. After this conference, Paul and Barnabas returned to Antioch with the decision and remained there for "some days," teaching and preaching with others.[135]

At that time, Paul decided to return to the churches they had previously planted to see how they were doing.[136] Barnabas was in agreement with the plan, but Paul and Barnabas got into a sharp dispute. Since they couldn't come to an agreement, Barnabas took Mark to Cyprus while Paul took Silas through Syria and Cilicia to strengthen the churches there. It is interesting that God was able to use this dispute to send two teams to strengthen the churches and encourage the groups of believers who had been planted and established on the "first missionary journey" in Acts 13–14.[137]

During this season of ministry, Paul found a new ministry partner, Timothy. He was focused on delivering the decrees that had been decided on by the elders and apostles in Jerusalem, on edifying the churches, and checking on their condition. As a result, the churches were strengthened and were increasing daily.[138]

The second journey did not end with simply strengthening the churches. After seeing they were well, Paul and his ministry team were led by the Holy Spirit to take the gospel farther. They passed through the Phrygian and Galatian region[139] after being forbidden by the Holy Spirit to preach in Asia, who then led them to Mysia and again restricted their plans by not allowing them to enter Bithynia. After passing through Mysia, they traveled to Troas, where Paul received a vision calling them to minister in Macedonia. They set out as soon as they were able from Troas, taking a

---

[135] Acts 15:30–36.

[136] Acts 15:36.

[137] The region of Pamphylia (where Perga and Attalia were) is absent from the description, but it is possible that Barnabas and Mark visited these regions after passing through the cities on Cyprus, just as Paul and Barnabas did on their first trip. Barnabas was not mentioned again in Acts after parting ways with Paul, so we do not have an inspired record of his continuing activities.

[138] Acts 16:1–5.

[139] For a good discussion of the possible views, the North and South Galatian theories, and the interaction between the Jerusalem decrees and the problems faced in the churches in Galatia, see Guthrie, *New Testament Introduction*, 465–86.

straight course to Samothrace, moving to Neapolis, and then to Philippi, where they stayed for some time.[140]

We have the record of Lydia's conversion to Christ, the first in Macedonia, in the leading city of Philippi. During their ministry, Paul confronted a slave girl who possessed a spirit of divination and cast a spirit out. This caused the masters of this slave girl to have Paul arrested. After God performed a miracle during Paul's and Silas's imprisonment, Paul had the chance to preach the gospel to the jailer, who repented and put his trust in Jesus. By the time the ruckus settled down in Philippi, a small community of believers had been formed and were meeting in Lydia's house.

After strengthening the congregation, Paul and his team traveled to Thessalonica and then to Berea, where Paul left Silas and Timothy, then to Athens and Corinth, where Silas and Timothy rejoined him. Paul settled in Corinth and met Priscilla and Aquila; he stayed there for a year and a half until trouble arose.[141] Paul began his trip back home to Antioch and sailed from Corinth with Priscilla and Aquila for Syria (where Antioch is), going first to Cenchrea, then to Ephesus, then to Caesarea, then to Jerusalem to greet the church,[142] and finally to Antioch.

Once again, Paul stayed some time in Antioch. He left to strengthen the churches that had been formed along the same route as previously—from

---

[140] Acts 16:6–12. The observant reader will notice the switch in pronouns used by Luke, the author of Acts, in 16:10 from "they" to "we." It is likely that Luke joined Paul's ministry team in Troas and accompanied Paul into Macedonia.

[141] Acts 18:18 says "Paul, having remained many days longer" after describing the ruckus in Corinth. It is difficult to say for sure, but the previous statement that he was there for a year and six months (Acts 18:11) precedes the trouble, and the following statement seems to indicate that Paul was in Corinth "many days" longer than that, staying even after the trouble arose before finally leaving. Many commentators simply say Paul stayed in Corinth for a year and a half based on Acts 18:11.

[142] Jerusalem is not mentioned in the locations listed in Acts 18:18–22. However, the terminology of "going up" in 18:22 is a figure of speech that refers to heading toward Jerusalem, and then "going down" as leaving from Jerusalem to Antioch. The Greek words for "going up" (ἀναβαίνω, *anabainō*) and "going down" (καταβαίνω, *katabainō*) are used not in reference to typical north and south directions but in relationship to going to or away from Jerusalem; see, e.g., Acts 15:2, 18:22, 21:12–15, 25:1.

Antioch through the Galatian region and Phrygia. That time, however, Paul was not hindered from entering Asia by the Holy Spirit, so his journey brought him back to Ephesus, where he spent the longest known time at any one location—three years.[143]

Paul's ministry in Ephesus was particularly fruitful; as a result, everyone in Asia, Jew and Gentile alike, heard the Word of the Lord.[144] Paul sent Timothy and Erastus to Macedonia before he traveled through Macedonia and eventually getting to Greece[145] and then returning after three months through Macedonia on his way back to Jerusalem to deliver the funds he had collected for the Jerusalem church.[146] Paul was arrested in Jerusalem; the events that led to his being transported to Rome and martyrdom were set in motion.

What is interesting in recalling Paul's ministry is the amount of time and attention he spent edifying the local churches and making sure they were strong and healthy. Some of Paul's letters were addressed to churches he had planted that were experiencing difficulties (for example, the Corinthian correspondence and the letter to the churches in Galatia). He wrote others (such as Thessalonians) to encourage and answer questions for churches that were doing pretty well. Paul wrote some letters to churches he had not visited but were planted as a result of the ongoing fruit of his work (for example, Colossians). As a result of Paul's focus on building up the church and local churches, he delegated responsibilities to other leaders who were able to increase the impact of Paul's ministry well beyond his own ability.

Paul left Priscilla and Aquila in Ephesus, where they mentored Apollos, who then went to Corinth and made an impact. Paul met Epaphras

---

[143] Acts 20:31. Recall that Paul stopped briefly at Ephesus on his return home to Antioch during the second journey, where he left Priscilla and Aquila. Paul told the Ephesians he would return if the Lord was willing (Acts 18:19–21).

[144] Acts 19:10.

[145] It is difficult to know for certain, but the reference to "Greece" is most likely referring to the same region as Achaia, where Corinth is. It is my position that Paul was in Corinth during Acts 20:2–3.

[146] See 1 Cor 16:1–4; 2 Cor 8:1—9:15; Rom 15:25–29.

somewhere along the line; he was in prison with Paul when he wrote to Philemon,[147] and he planted the church at Colossae, his hometown.[148]

Paul left Titus on Crete to oversee the churches there and to establish leadership,[149] and then he sent him all the way to Dalmatia (north of Macedonia) approximately five hundred miles away![150] Similarly, a ministry partner named Crescens was sent to Galatia,[151] perhaps to the northern region, which would have taken extra time and effort to reach with the gospel than was afforded when Paul had previously passed through that region.

Though Paul was never recorded as having visited Colossae, he wrote of the church there.

> We give thanks to God, the Father of our Lord Jesus Christ, praying always for you, since we heard of your faith in Christ Jesus and the love which you have for all the saints; because of the hope laid up for you in heaven, of which you previously heard in the word of truth, the gospel which has come to you, just as in all the world also it is constantly bearing fruit and increasing, even as it has been doing in you also since the day you heard of it and understood the grace of God in truth; just as you learned it from Epaphras, our beloved fellow bond-servant, who is a faithful servant of Christ on our behalf, and he also informed us of your love in the Spirit. (Col 1:3–8)

There was no hint of jealousy because they came to faith through the preaching of another—only thanksgiving and rejoicing as Paul heard of their faith in Christ and their love for the saints. Paul rejoiced because they had received the same type of faith, because they received it from a faithful brother, and because the gospel was constantly bearing fruit and

---

[147] Philm 1:23.

[148] Col 1:7, 4:12.

[149] Titus 1:4–5.

[150] 2 Tim 4:10.

[151] Ibid.

increasing in the entire world. Paul heard of their faith even though he had never been there.

Likewise, there is no record of Paul visiting any of the churches mentioned in Revelation other than Ephesus. Lydia, Paul's convert in Philippi, was from Thyatira. Perhaps she, like Epaphras, returned to her hometown to share the gospel. Unfortunately, it is unclear exactly how the Word of God spread and who took the Word where. While we may not know who brought the gospel, we know the church was active in fulfilling its responsibility to bring it to the ends of the earth. Despite not having every detail we might desire, we still have much to examine and draw conclusions from.

Perhaps most important, we are able to see how the Holy Spirit used Paul and his team to reach a vast geographical area with the gospel. The strategy was not always obvious to Paul, who sometimes found his plans being radically altered by the leading of the Holy Spirit. With hindsight, we can see Paul was an avid preacher of the gospel, but not just that. Paul was led to preach the gospel and to form churches in a few key areas in any particular province; then he moved on because healthy, functioning churches were intended to have a wide-reaching impact.

Michael Green accurately observed,

> [Paul] seems to have made a point of setting up two or three centres of the faith in a province, and then passing on, and allowing the native enthusiasm and initiative of the converts to lead them to others whom they could win for Christ. Thus, in Macedonia, he preached in Thessalonica, Beroea and Philippi; in Achaea he won converts in Athens and Corinth; in Cyprus, Salmis and Paphos. The central importance of Ephesus attracted him so much that he spent two full years there, and the Word of God spread throughout the province of Asia. It was no doubt during this period that Colossae and Laodicea were evangelized, through the agency of those whom Paul had brought to faith. This provincial strategy proved extremely effective. …

He did not work intensively for long years in a single place, but set up light-bearing communities of men who had found salvation in Christ, who could thereafter be "the sign, earnest and instrument of God's total plan of salvation" in that province. That is how he can dare to say, "I have completed the preaching of the gospel of Christ from Jerusalem as far round as Illyricum ...

But now I have no further scope in these parts, and I have been longing for many years to visit you on my way to Spain." His preaching had been representative; each province had heard something of the gospel, and little Christian communities were planted there to continue the work.[152]

Likewise, Frank Viola noted,

Strikingly, to Paul's mind an entire province was evangelized if he planted a few churches in the central cities that belonged to it. When Paul wrote his letter to the Romans, he and his coworkers had planted fewer than twenty churches in Galatia, Greece, Asia Minor, and Rome. Yet according to Paul, the gospel had been "fully preached" from Jerusalem all the way to Rome.

In only ten years—with fewer than twenty Gentile churches on the planet—Paul felt that there was no further place for him to preach in the regions from Jerusalem to Rome. (Rom. 15:19–24 KJV)[153]

Is this not astounding? Paul's strategy of church planting was so effective that he could say with integrity that after planting fewer than twenty

---

[152] Green, *Evangelism in the Early Church*, 263.
[153] Viola, *Finding Organic Church*, 47.

churches in a region that spanned more than 650,000 square miles, he had exhausted his scope and it was time to move on to different regions. To put this in perspective, I currently live in a city that spans less than five square miles, and we have at least thirty-three churches that hold weekend services.

Similarly, Paul ministered in Ephesus for approximately three years,[154] and the entire region was evangelized with everyone living there hearing the Word of the Lord as a result of his ministry after only two years.[155] Our local church was planted about one year ago in our area; we have gone door to door and spent a fair amount of time evangelizing in the marketplaces and downtown areas. It is astonishing how many people we meet who have never heard the basic content of the gospel. We have had churches in this area for decades, but still, the people are perishing in ignorance of the gospel.

How can this be? It is because our churches are of a completely different kind and quality than Paul's churches were. Don't misunderstand me; I am not saying believers today are somehow less saved than earlier Christians, nor am I saying the Holy Spirit is doing something different today from what he did in the early church. Instead, I am saying *we* are doing something different; we have drifted and have nullified the Word of God for our human traditions. We have attempted to modify God's design. In the process, we have largely quenched the Spirit of the living God by going our own way and building our mini-kingdoms of denominationalism instead of living for the glory of our God, who saved us, and the building of his kingdom. We have traded God's program for our programs that cater to the flesh and the world. If we are to have any hope of revitalizing the power of God in our churches today, we must repent and return to God's program.

---

[154] Acts 20:31.
[155] Acts 19:10.

CHAPTER 5

The Program

*But thanks be to God, who always leads us in triumph
in Christ, and manifests through us the sweet aroma
of the knowledge of Him in every place.*
—2 Corinthians 2:14

The division in our churches is perhaps most evident in the competition to bring the best, most complete set of programs to their communities. We have no shortage of programs; we have programs for children, youth, young adults, regular adults, senior adults, singles, married people, and the divorced. We have music programs, motorcycle programs, discipleship programs, addiction programs, prison programs, visitation programs, evangelism programs, shut-in programs, summer programs, winter programs, holiday programs, and so on. You name it, we have a program for it.

Did I miss your favorite program? Would you leave my church because I did not have it? I am not trying to be silly; this is a serious concern. People attend and leave churches because of their programs. Even when a church has a program, it is constantly in danger of losing people to a better program down the road or striving to improve its program beyond the other "competing" churches to boost attendance. As a result, many of the growing churches are growing by transfer growth, not through genuine conversions of nonbelievers.

This programmatic emphasis is at least partially responsible for the impotence of so many of our fellowships. After looking at the potency of Paul's churches and the incredible impact they had in reaching their regions with the gospel of Jesus Christ, we should realize he did not build churches by establishing thriving children's ministries. Never do you read of Paul exhorting believers to hire dynamic youth pastors or fail to grow. Likewise, Paul never encouraged his churches to make sure they had dynamic pastors with degrees from accredited universities. And he never mentioned the importance of talented music ministers.

So what did Paul point to? He made an amazing statement in his letter to the believers in Corinth: "Therefore I exhort you, be imitators of me. For this reason I have sent to you Timothy, who is my beloved and faithful child in the Lord, and he will remind you of my ways which are in Christ, just as I teach everywhere in every church" (1 Cor 4:16–17). This church was experiencing significant disunity and was tolerating sexual immorality.[156] Paul's encouragement to them to imitate him and hold fast to the traditions they had received was repeated in 1 Corinthians 11:1–2. The reality that he taught this everywhere in every church should grab our attention.

As we examine Paul's ways, we can see that he did not establish program-driven churches; he never took surveys of the felt needs of the community. We have no record of his using resources to create fun, no-strings-attached programs to appeal to the unchurched. Instead, Paul told his readers clearly what his program was in the opening chapter of 1 Corinthians.

> For Christ did not send me to baptize, but to preach the gospel, not in cleverness of speech, so that the cross of Christ would not be made void. For the word of the cross is foolishness to those who are perishing, but to us who are being saved it is the power of God. For it is written, "I will destroy the wisdom of the wise, and the cleverness of the clever I will set aside." Where is the wise man? Where is the scribe? Where is the debater of this age? Has not God made foolish the wisdom of the world? For since in the wisdom of God the world through its wisdom did not come to know God, God was well-pleased through the foolishness of the message preached to save those

---

[156] 1 Cor 1:10–13, 5:12.

who believe. For indeed Jews ask for signs and Greeks search for wisdom; but we preach Christ crucified, to Jews a stumbling block and to Gentiles foolishness, but to those who are the called, both Jews and Greeks, Christ the power of God and the wisdom of God. Because the foolishness of God is wiser than men, and the weakness of God is stronger than men. (1 Cor 1:17–25)

By the apostle's own description, Christ had not sent him to establish programs but to preach the gospel. He knew what the Jews wanted—signs. He knew what the Greeks wanted—wisdom. What was his response? He preached a crucified Messiah; his message was the power and wisdom of God to those who believed. This same message was foolishness to the rest. He didn't give them what they wanted or felt they needed. Paul instead chose to give them what Christ had said they needed. He didn't give them the best programs he could built with the material resources available to him and upon the backs of volunteers. Paul instead gave them the pure gospel built on the power of God.

Despite modern ideas, God's power does not rely upon programs, methods, or resources; it does not rely on hiring a dynamic speaker, someone with a PhD, or being culturally "relevant." God's power and wisdom are found in the gospel.

Paul gave us a further description of his ways in Christ as he continued his correspondence with the Corinthians. In the first six chapters of 1 Corinthians, Paul dealt with matters they were not interested in him addressing. Paul had heard from Chloe's people about the division, sexual immorality, and lawsuits among Christians, and he addressed these problems head-on. However, it seems that the delegation from Chloe was sent with specific questions that Paul answered starting in chapter 7, using the repeated phrase "now concerning" and discussing matters pertaining to divorce, (re)marriage, being single, Christian liberty, the idolatry and folly of Israel, authority and order in the church and home, the Lord's Supper, and the proper use of spiritual gifts and their exercise in the church.

Due to the sheer number of problems he was addressing, it is easy to miss Paul's little statement about imitating his ways, holding firm the traditions, and the reality that he taught that in every church. We can look back and see how Paul consistently went to strategic places to proclaim the glory of the gospel, first to Jew and then to Gentile, in accordance with his calling and stewardship God entrusted to him. We can see that Paul encouraged and strengthened these churches after his bold, faithful, and loving proclamation of the gospel, trusting they could sustain the same ministry of faithfully proclaiming this message to others.

When Epaphras did this to his hometown of Colossae, Paul rejoiced and wrote to this community, which he had never met, with confidence they were sharing in the ministry of evangelizing the world—because that is God's program to the praise and glory of his name and grace. He wrote to them assuming they participated in the same ministry program he did.

> We proclaim Him, admonishing every man and teaching every man with all wisdom, so that we may present every man complete in Christ. For this purpose also I labor, striving according to His power, which mightily works within me. (Col 1:28–29)

Paul included these saints in Colossae in the ministry of proclaiming Christ, admonishing[157] and teaching everyone with the purpose of presenting them in Christ before the Father. They also participated with him in the same labor he strove for in God's power.

In contrast to the believers in Colossae, Paul was careful to remind the believers in Corinth of the truth of the gospel in chapter 15, and he discussed some important theology regarding the resurrection. We must not miss what he wrote in verse 34: "Become sober-minded as you ought, and stop sinning; for some have no knowledge of God. I speak this to your shame." Paul revealed the primary reason for his desire they should stop sinning; it was not because their sinning was making them unhappy, and it was not for some self-interested reason. Instead, Paul told them they

---

[157] The word translated as *admonish* is νουθετέω (*noytheteō*) and is defined in BDAG as "to counsel about avoidance or cessation of an improper course of conduct, *admonish, warn, instruct*" (italics in original). Warning people about the terrifying consequences of failing to heed the Lord's command to all men, everywhere to repent and believe the gospel is part of the Christian call (e.g., Acts 17:30–31).

should have been ashamed of themselves because there were some who had no knowledge of God. Their sin was distracting them from their primary duty as Christians—spreading the knowledge of God through the gospel and the testimony of the church.

Paul returned to this theme in 2 Corinthians as he once again described his apostolic ministry.

> But thanks be to God, who always leads us in triumph in Christ, and manifests through us the sweet aroma of the knowledge of Him in every place. For we are a fragrance of Christ to God among those who are being saved and among those who are perishing; to the one an aroma from death to death, to the other an aroma from life to life. And who is adequate for these things? (2 Cor 2:14–16)

Paul's commitment to going where the Spirit led him to manifest the knowledge of God is truly awe inspiring.

Paul met opposition in Corinth; he faced challengers to his apostolic authority. It is difficult to discern the exact nature of the accusations (since we don't have them in writing), but we can at least get the gist from Paul's responses to them. One of the issues Paul dealt with in 2 Corinthians 1:12—2:11 was the charge that he walked according to his flesh, was double-minded, and was acting in accordance with what was beneficial for himself over and above those he claimed to minister to. But he sought to follow the lead of the Holy Spirit, to do all things for the sake of the gospel and the glory of God, and to do all things for the edification of the church. When circumstances changed that would bring challenges to his plans of bringing glory to God, advancing the gospel, and edifying the church, Paul was not afraid to change his plans. In that, he was single-minded. That single-minded devotion in these matters was why Paul described his thanksgiving even in the midst of things not going the way he had envisioned and planned in 2 Corinthians 2:12–13 because God always leads Christians in triumph in Christ and manifests through us the sweet aroma of the knowledge of Jesus everywhere. At least, God does this when we become sober minded and stop sinning. Sin can detract us from our God-ordained purpose to manifest the knowledge of God, but when we are walking in accordance with his will, God works through us for that purpose. It is why God saved us.

The results of manifesting the knowledge of God are important since it is multifaceted. It has an aspect in relationship to God, another in relationship to those who are perishing, and a third to those who are being saved.

First, in relationship to God, when we manifest the knowledge of Jesus wherever we are, 2 Corinthians 2:15 tells us we are a fragrance of Christ to God among those who are being saved and among those who are perishing. The Bible has no problem dividing the world into two categories—Jew and Gentile, light and dark, children of God and children of the Devil, those who are being saved and those who are perishing. What this passage says is that regardless of the people to whom the knowledge of God is being manifested—whether they are being saved or whether they are perishing—walking in God's program of manifesting the knowledge of Jesus is a pleasing fragrance to God the Father.

Do you get this? No matter how people respond to the gospel, God the Father is pleased when Jesus is proclaimed. God was pleased when Peter spoke the gospel and three thousand souls were saved. God was pleased when Stephen proclaimed the gospel and they murdered him where he stood. Different responses, same gospel. Different responses from the crowd, same response from God; he was pleased as if he had been smelling a pleasing aroma.

The text also tells us that the reactions of the people to Christians manifesting the sweet aroma of the knowledge of Jesus will be different based on their situations. The second aspect of this manifestation of the knowledge of God is for those who are perishing: it is an aroma from death to death; the longer this knowledge is manifested, the worse it seems to get for those who are perishing. Have you ever been in a place that had a bad smell? It can be tough to bear. When I leased apartments, I learned the power of odors. No one wants to live in a place that stinks. Smells are powerful.

The imagery Paul used is vivid. He went beyond saying that hearing about God is unpleasant to those who are perishing to saying that the more those who are perishing hear about the true and living God, the worse it gets for them. It is like a foul odor that grows in strength like a skunk's smell that gets stronger as you near ground zero. Since Paul was so adamant about his calling to manifest the knowledge of God everywhere he went, no wonder we see him frequently getting chased out of cities. The longer he stayed, the worse his stink became to those who were perishing.

Of course, there is a third and final aspect of this program. Among those who are being saved, manifesting the knowledge of God is an aroma from life to life; it gets better and better. I liken this to when my wife cooks something in the crockpot and the smell begins to permeate the house. The first whiff smells pretty good, but as mealtime approaches, it gets even better and ends up being irresistible.

It should be the same for followers of Christ who have the knowledge of God. When we first start to get to know God, we find he is more amazing and awesome than we could have realized. However, this knowledge keeps getting better and better! The more I hear about the glory of God in the gospel, the more amazing it becomes.

Is that true for you? It should be. The more we get to know God, the more he should consume our thoughts. Born-again Christians should be moving steadily toward a place where they can think of little else other than God, who lives and reigns and who gave his only begotten Son to be a propitiation for sin. What else is there?

This program of God using his children to manifest the knowledge of who he is in the world is in line with the theology of the church as described by our leading theologians. This was no small theme in Paul's writings. In the epistle to the Galatians, Paul wrote of his astonishment that they were turning from the gospel they had received to another gospel, which was no gospel at all. Paul also used the strongest language possible when he declared that those preaching a different gospel were to be accursed with everlasting condemnation in hell.[158] In the process of turning to a different gospel, the Galatians were turning away from the person of God.[159] Paul urged these Christians to walk with the Spirit of the living God because they knew God and were known by him.[160]

To the saints in Ephesus, Paul wrote of the glory of God's plan to give to his children a spirit of wisdom and of revelation in the knowledge

[158] Gal 1:8–9.
[159] For more on this, see Kohler, *Gate Crashers*, 56–70.
[160] Gal 3:3; 4:8–9; 5:1–26.

of him.[161] Paul prayed that they would be unified in the faith and in the knowledge of the Son of God.[162] Paul prayed that the believers in Colossae would be filled with a knowledge of God's will so they would walk in a manner worthy of the Lord, please him in all respects, bear fruit in every good work, and increase in the knowledge of God.[163] Paul expressed his desire for these saints to have a full assurance of understanding that would result from a knowledge of Christ.[164]

Paul explained to the believers in Thessalonica how their knowledge of God led to their sanctification in contrast to those who lived in accordance with their lusts because they didn't know God.[165] Similarly, Paul warned Titus of the empty confession of those who claimed to know God but whose deeds demonstrated they did not.[166] He further warned the Thessalonians of the dreadful consequences coming upon those who did not know God in contrast to the glorious hope for those who did.[167]

Paul wrote to the saints in Rome that God's judgment was upon the unbelievers because they suppressed what was known about God in their unrighteousness.[168] Paul understood that the world was not able to come to know God on its own, so God was pleased to have people come to know him through the proclamation of the gospel.[169] Since the knowledge of God was manifested through Christians, Paul took the proclamation of the gospel seriously and sought to tear down anything that was raised up against the knowledge of God.[170] This included admonishing those in sin, because sin in the lives of believers caused them to lose focus on God's program of manifesting the knowledge of Christ in every place.

Paul wrote to Timothy of God's desire that all be saved and come to a knowledge of the truth—a knowledge of the one mediator between God

---

[161] Eph 1:17.
[162] Eph 4:13.
[163] Col 1:9–10.
[164] Col 2:1–3.
[165] 1 Thess 4:2–5.
[166] Titus 1:16.
[167] 2 Thess 1:6–12.
[168] Rom 1:18–19.
[169] 1 Cor 1:21; Rom 10:14–15, 16:25–27; 2 Cor 4:6.
[170] 2 Cor 10:3–6.

and humanity and what people must do to receive Christ as Savior.[171] Paul encouraged Timothy to remain faithful on the basis of Paul's knowing Jesus personally and knowing Jesus was faithful not just to Paul but also to Timothy.[172] Paul encouraged Timothy that this "knowledge" wasn't one-sided but that Jesus knew those who were his.[173]

Paul was not content simply to manifest the knowledge of God to others, or to pray that believers would know God better, or warn of the consequences coming to those who did not know God. Paul was not shy about professing to the Philippians his desire above all else to grow in his knowledge of God, which he viewed as having a value greater than anything else.[174]

Are you getting the picture? Paul was consumed with the knowledge of God. He wanted to know Christ, and he wanted others to know Christ. He wanted to destroy anything that would hinder people from coming to know Christ. He did everything so the knowledge of Christ could increase. He thanked God that even when his own circumstances were difficult or seemingly contrary to the good, the knowledge of Christ was expanding and that was a reason to celebrate.[175]

In light of this, how do you think Paul would react if the Corinthians had told him about their plan to hold nonconfrontational potlucks so the church could get to know members of the community? Do you think Paul would respond favorably to outreach and evangelism methods that prioritized human relationships horizontally over pointing people to the Savior so they could have a right relationship with God vertically? Many outreach and church-growth strategies recognize that the more we magnify Jesus, the reaction of death to death is still how those who are perishing react. However, if we prioritize our programs that cater to the various lusts and impulses of the flesh and the general brokenness of this present world and desire to numerically grow those who sow into our own ministry, diminishing Jesus and emphasizing felt needs becomes a

---

[171] 1 Tim 2:3–8.
[172] 2 Tim 1:8–13.
[173] 2 Tim 2:19.
[174] Phil 3:8–12.
[175] E.g., Phil 1:12–20.

reasonable strategy. Not biblical, but reasonable.[176] We can justify this strategy because the people we supposedly want to reach seemingly respond much better because they are willing to participate in the programs we've created to minister to their felt needs, whereas they do not respond with pleasure to the preaching of the gospel.

After examining this theme in greater detail, let us return to what Paul said to the Corinthians.

> Therefore I exhort you, be imitators of me. For this reason I have sent to you Timothy, who is my beloved and faithful child in the Lord, and he will remind you of my ways which are in Christ, just as I teach everywhere in every church. (1 Cor 4:16–17)

Imitators of Paul—who sought to proclaim boldly, faithfully, and lovingly the gospel of Jesus. Imitators of Paul—who lived to know Jesus and to make him known. Imitators of Paul—who lived to tear down anything that hindered a saving knowledge of Jesus Christ. Not only this, but to understand that such a ministry is pleasing to God and pleasing to those who are being saved but is displeasing to those who are perishing.

As a result, Paul knew that persecution was waiting for him everywhere he went not simply because he was an apostle but because this was the nature of Christian ministry. If we do it well and manifest the knowledge of God, persecution awaits us too. Paul was not kidding when he warned young Timothy, "Indeed, all who desire to live godly in Christ Jesus will be persecuted" (2 Tim 3:12). Not might be. Will be. When we cater to the flesh and stop seeking to make Jesus known in all his fullness, persecution is not necessary. No one persecutes Christians for having nonconfrontational potlucks.

We should be alarmed that we have found a way to "share Jesus" with people without it either being an aroma of life to life or an aroma of death to death. Somehow, we have so modified the program of God, watered down the message of the gospel, and hidden the knowledge of God that ambivalence is a normal response. Christians are not being persecuted in the United States as they are in other places. It is not because we are a

---

[176] Prov 14:12; 16:25; Gal 2:20.

Christian nation; it has already been stated that some statistics indicate the United States has the third-largest population of unreached nonbelievers on earth.[177]

The reality is that we have substituted the program (singular) God intends for his church to follow with programs (plural) that appeal to the flesh of nonbelievers and immature Christians. We spend more time trying to get people to know each other than we do urging them to get to know God. In many cases, people are preaching and teaching caricatures of God that skew the character of the living God revealed in the Scriptures and who walked the earth in the person of Jesus Christ—the God who is coming again in glory to gather a people to himself from every tribe, tongue, and nation and to crush his adversaries under his feet.

Do you know God? Are you making him known? If you're not doing the second, it is possible you don't truly know him. This may seem harsh, but the stakes are too high to worry about hurting others' feelings and letting them perish under the wrath of God.[178] Charles Wesley aptly stated, "To tell one in darkness he has faith is to keep him in darkness still, or to make him trust in false light, a faith that stands in the words of men, not in the power of God."[179] God's love in us should compel us to proclaim the good news to everyone on earth. Lindsell rightly stated,

> God has no other agency whose duty it is to fulfill the terms of the Great Commission. If the church does not fulfill its destiny the gospel will not be preached. And God has made no other plans. Even the angels cannot preach the gospel. This is reserved for the church of Jesus Christ alone.[180]

---

[177] Payne, *Unreached Peoples*. E-book available from www.jdpayne.org/wp-content/uploads/2014/02/Unreached-Peoples-Least-Reached-Places-Payne.pdf. Accessed November 18, 2015.

[178] Paul Washer's *Gospel Assurance & Warnings* is an excellent resource for anyone who wants to take seriously the biblical counsel on examining ourselves to see if we are in the faith (2 Cor 13:5). I encourage every professing Christian to read this excellent book and to prayerfully consider the truth it contains.

[179] Kimbrough and Newport, *Manuscript Journal*, 2:350–51.

[180] Lindsell, "Biblical Basis of Missions," 149.

As we grow in the grace and knowledge of Jesus, we should likewise grow in our understanding that we exist to manifest the knowledge of God everywhere. We will turn our attention in the next chapter to the biblical testimony on the love of God.

Tom—A Testimony

(Tom is a senior applications engineer. He personally shares the gospel with hundreds to thousands of individuals per year regularly.)

For years, I considered myself a pretty good Christian. I attended church every week and got up early to read the Bible and pray every day. However, I always knew I was lacking in the area of sharing the gospel. It wasn't that I thought I needed to do anything crazy like going out and talking to strangers on the street or standing somewhere in public and proclaiming the gospel; I just knew I always passed up opportunities to talk to friends, family, and coworkers about Jesus and Christianity.

To say that I'm a pretty quiet and reserved guy is a tremendous understatement. Most people who know me would tell you that. On top of that, I'm an engineer, and many of my friends and coworkers are also very logical and scientifically minded. Based on these two factors (my own personality and the personalities of most of the people I know), I let opportunity after opportunity to share the gospel pass by because I felt intimidated. I felt I could never win any debate if we were to talk about God vs. evolution, etc. I thought that if I learned more apologetics, I would develop the confidence to enter those debates. So I invested the time and studied those things more.

But nothing really changed. I continued like this for a number of years until my church offered a class called The Way of the Master.[181] I saw the promo video and got excited about it because it claimed to be able to show how to share the gospel in a logical and systematic way that didn't seem to rely on debating and all the other things that intimidated me. Pastor Joe did an excellent job teaching the material, and I was certainly prepared to share the gospel.

However, what I found out was that it wasn't necessarily the lack of

---

[181] www.wayofthemaster.com.

knowledge that kept me from sharing the gospel; it was just plain old fear. Because a number of others were in the class, I got through the class without having to really do the things I was scared to do. I hid my fear; I learned the material but did not put it into practice.

As I sat in church over the next couple of years, I heard many sermons about how Christ commanded us to preach the gospel to the lost. I knew (and still know) lots of nonbelievers. I have a great concern for them and their eternal well-being. I knew I had the knowledge and tools to share the gospel with them, and I could feel the Holy Spirit convicting me to do it, but I still let my fear choke this conviction out and continued to disobey God's command to proclaim the gospel to every creature. So when The Way of the Master was offered again, I signed up again. This time, the class was being led by our staff evangelist, Joel. I confessed to him I was signing up again because I had not put what I'd learned the first time into practice. I knew he wouldn't let me get away with that.

Joel did indeed keep me accountable and helped me put theory into practice. He made it very clear that the entire class would stay on a particular lesson until everyone completed the assignment for that week. Having been through the class before, I knew that wouldn't be too much of a problem until the last couple of weeks; that is when the assignments were to hand out gospel tracts and share the gospel with someone in conversation. Joel led us through role-playing in class and took us out individually to watch how he put the things we were learning into practice in his own witnessing.

It finally came time for me to go out and share the gospel. I wanted so badly to back out, but I knew Joel wouldn't let me, and I didn't want to sit in church weekly hearing the conviction of the Holy Spirit and not do anything about it. So with knees knocking and voice shaking, I went out and shared the gospel on the street with a stranger for the first time.

I would like to say all my fears went away after that first time, but they didn't. I probably would have been content to be able to say I'd done it and go back to just sitting in church again. However, even after the class ended, Joel continued to encourage me to go out with him and others who had been through the class.

Because our evangelist was free to lead our body in the external call to evangelize the whole world (starting with our community), he never let the momentum stop. Now, I go out with a group of guys just about every Saturday and Sunday to share the gospel with people in our community. I have been to Chicago, Indianapolis, and Los Angeles in addition to other cities in my home state on witnessing trips with these same guys as well. I have even stood in public areas and proclaimed the gospel a few times to passers-by.

I still feel the prodding of the Holy Spirit, but now, it is to share the gospel more and more. This is much different from knowing I am disobeying the Lord's command to go altogether. I know God is glorified when a shy person such as myself proclaims his glorious gospel message to people. If God can do it in and through me, he can do it in anyone who is willing to be used by him.

CHAPTER 6

For the Love of God

For the love of Christ controls us, having concluded this, that
one died for all, therefore all died; and He died for all, so
that they who live might no longer live for themselves, but
for Him who died and rose again on their behalf.
—2 Corinthians 5:14–15

Much can be and indeed has been said about God's love and the Christians' love for God. It is unlikely a single chapter could fully describe or express God's love, and this chapter won't try. Instead, we'll examine God's love as it pertains to the purpose of the church in proclaiming the gospel to the ends of the earth.

I have not often heard God's love and evangelism tied together, but that is not to say it doesn't happen. In his excellent work on evangelism in the early church, Michael Green stated,

> There can be little doubt that the main motive for evangelism [in the early church] was a theological one. These men did not spread their message because it was advisable for them to do so, nor because it was the socially responsible thing to do. They did not do it primarily for humanitarian or agathistic utilitarian reasons. They did it because of the overwhelming experience of the love of God which they had received through Jesus Christ. The discovery that the ultimate force in the universe was Love, and that this Love had stooped to the very nadir of

self-abasement for human good, had an effect on those who believed it which nothing could remove.[182]

Green pointed out two related items: theology and experience. He claimed the earliest followers of Jesus—who evangelized with power and saw amazing fruit from their tireless efforts and self-sacrificial love—were motivated mainly by a theological understanding of God's love. However, mere theological information was not enough. It was the "overwhelming experience" of this theological truth of God's love that they had received through Jesus and the indwelling Holy Spirit that proved to be an irresistible motivator for these followers of Jesus to risk life and limb for the glory of God and the benefit of others.

In this chapter, we can deal with the theological aspect. However, you are on your own for the experiential aspect. You can get information about someone by reading a biography, but you have to take additional steps to actually know that person. We can read the Bible and obtain information about God, but walking with him is another matter.

Green continued,

> In a word, Christian evangelism has its motivation rooted in what God is and what he has done for man through the coming and the death and the resurrection of Jesus. "We love because he first loved us." This is what Paul meant when he wrote that "the love of Christ grips us, because we are convinced that one has died for all; therefore all have died. And he died for all, that those who live might live no longer for themselves but for him who for their sake died and was raised."[183]

I agree with Green. Christian evangelism has its motivation rooted in God's nature and what he accomplished through Jesus Christ. I also know this view is not shared by everyone. Once, after I preached a particularly difficult message from the Word, a member of the congregation approached me and wanted to have a meeting. During the meeting, she expressed a

---

[182] Green, *Evangelism in the Early Church*, 236.
[183] Ibid., 237.

grave concern for me and a hope I would experience and understand the love of God.

Of course I was confused. *You don't think your pastor understands or experiences the love of God?* I thought. But as the meeting progressed, it became clear that she was worried about me because I did not always express a lot of emotion or at least did not in the way she considered the most appropriate to the passage. At the heart of her concern was the fact that I seemed to stress obedience to God, which she incorrectly asserted meant I was working to earn God's love and favor. I'd heard that more than once. Sometimes, people who hear my teaching think I emphasize obedience too much and don't spend enough time or attention on the more emotional aspects of Christian love. In fact, a number of professing Christians take issue with any teaching that emphasizes obedience in the life of a believer, applying the label of "legalism" without any hesitation.

It is true—I am not the best at expressing my emotions. I sometimes joke with my wife that I have only two emotions—angry and hungry. When she tells me the second one is not really an emotion, I tend to experience the first one. My excuse is that I'm a male, so emotional awareness is not one of my strengths. (Certainly, some men are more in touch with their emotions and feelings than others.) However, I have wept during many worship services in response to various emotions overtaking me. I have wept in my prayer closet over the people I am leading as a result of sin and tragedy but also joy. While I appreciate the concern that was expressed, when I evaluate my own walk with the Lord, I am not concerned with a lack of emotion.

Yet does the Bible teach that the love of God should cause us to be overly emotional? Is this the best indicator of our genuine participation in the love of God? Are we instructed by the Word to judge our love for him by how loud we sing in worship services or by how high we raise our hands? Is the love of God in our lives measured by the tingly feeling we get when we worship or based on whether we jump up and down during the music time? That seems more like the cultural definition of love than the biblical definition. *Love*, like *church*, is one of those words people bring their own definitions to and read into the Scriptures. What does the Bible have to say about love? Some say the best definition of love is in 1 Corinthians;

you know the passage. Anyone who has ever been to a wedding has almost certainly heard it.

> Love is patient, love is kind and is not jealous; love does not brag and is not arrogant, does not act unbecomingly; it does not seek its own, is not provoked, does not take into account a wrong suffered, does not rejoice in unrighteousness, but rejoices with the truth; bears all things, believes all things, hopes all things, endures all things. Love never fails. (1 Cor 13:4–8a)

This is an undoubtedly beautiful passage. Everything it says is true, good, and right. However, it has nothing to do with weddings. It also doesn't mention warm, fuzzy feelings or overpowering emotions. The context of this passage is the proper use of spiritual gifts in the church. This is not *the* definition of love; it was intended to be an edifying instruction on the loving and proper use of spiritual gifts in the corporate gathering.

Love is definitely this. It is also more than this. This passage speaks about love as applied to the exercise of spiritual gifts in the body. But how about love as applied to God? The apostle John is sometimes referred to as the apostle of love. His transformation is amazing to see as he was changed by the grace of God over time. When Mark described the appointment of the twelve by Jesus, he recorded that Jesus gave John and his brother James the name Boanerges, "Sons of Thunder."[184] This is the same James and John who came to Jesus and asked to sit at his right and left in glory,[185] the same John who tried to prevent someone from ministering in the name of Jesus because he wasn't a part of the group,[186] and the same James and John who asked Jesus if he wanted them to command fire to come down and consume some Samaritans who had refused to receive Jesus as he traveled toward Jerusalem.[187] Son of Thunder to apostle of love—quite a transformation indeed.

John spoke of God's great love for those who were in Christ and what

---

[184] Mark 3:17.
[185] Mark 10:35–41.
[186] Luke 9:49.
[187] Luke 9:54.

it meant to love God. He defined the love of God clearly: "For this is the love of God, that we keep His commandments; and His commandments are not burdensome" (1 John 5:3). John also wrote the amazing declaration that God is love. Let's consider this passage in its surrounding context.

John began by exhorting Christians to love one another: "Beloved, let us love one another, for love is from God; and everyone who loves is born of God and knows God. The one who does not love does not know God, for God is love" (1 John 4:7–8). As John was writing to Christians, he asserted that they were called to love one another. Perhaps more important, he asserted that the source of this love was God. Our love for fellow Christians is not related to our satisfaction or appreciation of our brothers and sisters in Christ per se but is an overflow of God's love being poured out on us. John pointed out that the presence of love was evidence of our being born again and of our knowledge of or relationship with the living God. If love is lacking, this is proof we do not know God.

John explained what God's love really was.

> By this the love of God was manifested in us, that God has sent His only begotten Son into the world so that we might live through Him. In this is love, not that we loved God, but that He loved us and sent His Son to be the propitiation for our sins. (1 John 4:9–10)

God's love was manifested by the reality that when we were in rebellion against him, the Father sent Jesus to save us. When God declared we must love our enemies, he was telling us to do what he had done first. We know what love is only by understanding the nature of God's sacrifice. Love is not simply about overwhelming emotions; it is a choice. Love includes action. God sent his Son to be the propitiation for our sins when God's wrath was still upon us. There were strong, passionate feelings at work there, but not warm, fuzzy ones.

Propitiation is a doctrine that is losing focus in the professing church. When I meet professing Christians while evangelizing, I will often ask them what some guy who died two thousand years ago has to do with me. This is an opportunity for them to explain to me the doctrine of propitiation. Sadly, the vast majority I meet have no idea what Jesus was really doing on the cross. As a result, according to John, they do not really understand what God's love is; it is in the sending of his Son to be the propitiation for our sins that we see God's love manifested.

The lack of understanding of the doctrine of propitiation explains why many professing Christians think everything is okay with their friends, family members, and coworkers who believe in God and pray. I hear even professing Christians encourage unbelievers to pray to God as if this is a helpful step on the path to spirituality. I drive by a church that recently had this on its sign: "Need someone to listen? Just pray." Who is this sign for? Are nonbelievers really being encouraged to "just pray" to God? In their own name and righteousness?[188] These notions betray a severe misunderstanding of God's revealed nature. When humanity rebelled against God, he cursed it with death. The breach in the relationship between God and humanity is no small matter.

And it is not one-sided. We were born into rebellion against God; we willfully participate in this rebellion with every word, breath, and deed. By nature, we are born as children of wrath.[189] This is how God can justly condemn the world and how his judgment declares that every intention of the human heart is evil.[190] In his holiness, God does not overlook this rebellion and wickedness; his wrath and indignation burn toward both sin and sinner.[191] Humanity turned its back on God, and God turned his back on us. The existence of seemingly happy thoughts toward whatever idea of "god" some rebellious sinners may have does nothing to change God's disposition toward those who sin.

God will by no means leave the guilty unpunished.[192] This is why the doctrine of propitiation is so glorious and so important. What we could never do, God did by sending his Son in the likeness of sinful flesh— though Jesus himself knew no sin—to suffer under the wrath of God the Father, taking the curse upon himself.[193] Jesus submitted himself to this

---

[188] Cf. Prov 28:9; John 14:6.

[189] Eph 2:1–3.

[190] Gen 6:5, 8:21; Rom 3:10, 23, 6:23. For a more detailed discussion of this, see Kohler, *Gate Crashers*, 24–34 and 193–203.

[191] E.g., Pss 5:5, 7:11–12; Nah 1:2–8; John 3:36; 2 Thess 1:6–10; Heb 10:26–31; Rev 19:11–16.

[192] Exod 34:7; Jer 30:11, 46:28; Nah 1:3.

[193] Rom 8:1–4; 2 Cor 5:21; Gal 3:13; Isa 53:1–12.

in fulfillment of God's predetermined plan[194] to satisfy God's wrath and uphold his justice.[195] When Jesus took our sins upon himself and defeated death, sin, and hell through his triumphant resurrection from the dead, he made it possible for God's wrath to be satisfied and for God's favor to be freely and lavishly bestowed upon those who were formerly God's enemies through our wicked works.[196]

What we could never earn, God freely gave. And what God gave was most precious in his sight.[197] What amazing love! If we have been redeemed by our God and experienced this lavish, extravagant love firsthand, how can that love not flow to others? John answered this simply: it must. If it does not, the love of God is not in us.

Understanding God's great love for us compels us to love one another. In 4:11–16, John took this a step further to define this love in more detail.

> Beloved, if God so loved us, we also ought to love one another. No one has seen God at any time; if we love one another, God abides in us, and His love is perfected in us. By this we know that we abide in Him and He in us, because He has given us of His Spirit. We have seen and testify that the Father has sent the Son to be the Savior of the world. Whoever confesses that Jesus is the Son of God, God abides in him, and he in God. We have come to know and have believed the love which God has for us. God is love, and the one who abides in love abides in God, and God abides in him.

This love is expressed in Christians through their testimony regarding the Father sending the Son to be the Savior of the world. The text explicitly states that confessing Jesus is the Son of God to the world is evidence the person belongs to God and abides in him (1 John 4:14–15). Since God's

---

[194] Acts 2:23.

[195] Rom 3:21–26. For a more detailed description of this glorious passage, see Washer, *Gospel's Power & Message.*

[196] Rom 5:8–10; 2 Cor 5:21; Eph 2:8–9; Titus 3:4–8.

[197] 1 Pet 1:17–25.

love is manifested in sending Jesus to die for the sin of the world, Christian love should overflow in testifying of this great love to the world.

> By this, love is perfected with us, so that we may have confidence in the day of judgment; because as He is, so also are we in this world. There is no fear in love; but perfect love casts out fear, because fear involves punishment, and the one who fears is not perfected in love. We love, because He first loved us. If someone says, "I love God," and hates his brother, he is a liar; for the one who does not love his brother whom he has seen, cannot love God whom he has not seen. And this commandment we have from Him, that the one who loves God should love his brother also. (1 John 4:17–21)

John finished where he began with an admonition that the love of God was tied to a love of brother. He also made it explicit that love casts out fear. We can love because God loved us. We need not fear because God loved us. We must love others because God loved us. God's love, when experienced by the Christian, must overflow into a love for God and a love for others. Tied to this love is the explicit expectation that our love will manifest itself in the testimony of God's love by sending his Son to be the propitiation for our sins.

Love of God. Love for others. This sounds like Jesus's summary of the Law and the prophets, doesn't it?[198]

Once again, John recorded some helpful explanatory statements from Jesus as to what exactly it means to love him. Jesus taught, "If you love Me, you will keep My commandments" (John 14:15). According to Jesus, love was expressed through obedience to his Commandments. This obedience is not to earn his love but a reaction to his love. He loved us, so we ought to love him—whether we feel like it or not. Jesus repeated this same theme again in verses 21–24 of John 14. He added some cool promises to this explanation of what it meant to love him. Jesus promised that those who loved him and kept his Commandments would be loved by the Father and Jesus and that Jesus would make himself known to them. That's great

---

[198] E.g., Matt 22:37–40.

news!¹⁹⁹ Jesus also promised that he and the Father would dwell with those who loved God and kept his Commandments. Jesus also expressed the opposite side of this truth for completeness—those who do not love Jesus do not keep his words (John 14:24).

In the next chapter of John's gospel, Jesus reiterated the importance of abiding in his love and keeping his Commandments. Jesus then stated plainly his commandment was that his followers loved one another.[200] This love for one another was so important that Jesus proclaimed that the world would know we were his followers by our love for each other.[201]

Once again, we are confronted with the realities that God is love, Christians can only love because God first loved us, this love should overflow in a love for God and for others, and this love includes at least obeying Christ's Commandments and testifying of God's love expressed through Christ. Understanding this love was clearly important to Jesus and John and incredibly important to Paul. He wanted followers of Christ to be edified and to manifest the knowledge of God in every place; he found God's love to be indispensable.

Paul further prayed for the Ephesians

> that He would grant you, according to the riches of His glory, to be strengthened with power through His Spirit in the inner man, so that Christ may dwell in your hearts through faith; and that you, being rooted and grounded in love, may be able to comprehend with all the saints what is the breadth and length and height and depth, and to know the love of Christ which surpasses knowledge, that you may be filled up to all the fullness of God. (Eph 3:16–19)

For Paul, a genuine understanding of Christ's love was necessary for them being filled to the fullness of God.

---

[199] Especially considering the discussion in chapter 5.

[200] John 15:9–13.

[201] For an interesting discussion on the importance and effectiveness of Christian love expressed in the fellowship of believers as a powerful evangelistic force in the early church, see Green, *Evangelism in the Early Church*, 180–83.

To recap Paul's message through his letter to the saints in Ephesus: God designed his church to be the fullness of Christ on earth (Eph 1:23). God had an administration suitable to the fullness of the times that has been given through revelation (Eph 1:10, 3:1–13). In response to this revelation from the living God, Paul prayed that Christians would understand God's love so they would be filled up to all the fullness of God (Eph 3:19). Finally, the risen Christ gave some as apostles, some as prophets, some as evangelists, and some as pastors and teachers to equip and build up the body until they attained the measure of the stature that belongs to the fullness of Christ (Eph 4:11–13). Paul likewise included speaking the truth in love as part of the Christian maturation process (Eph 4:15). We must understand God's love and submit to the officers Christ gave as a gift to build up the body into its mature form.

So how did Paul understand God's love? Paul was gripped by Christ's love to proclaim the gospel boldly, faithfully, and lovingly.

> For the love of Christ controls us, having concluded this, that one died for all, therefore all died; and He died for all, so that they who live might no longer live for themselves, but for Him who died and rose again on their behalf. (2 Cor 5:14–15)

Commentators disagree over whether the phrase "the love of Christ" should be taken as an objective or as a subjective genitive; which is to say, is it our love for Christ or Christ's love for us that is in control? A case can be made either way, but perhaps the ambiguity was implied so we would not restrict it to one or the other. Christ's love for us should control us, and our love for him should control us; both should lead us to die to self and live for the praise and glory of his name. It is immediately on the heels of this statement that Paul declared the awesome privilege and responsibility that every Christian had been called to share in as ambassadors for Christ and ministers of reconciliation.[202]

The love of Christ brings us back to evangelism—Jesus taught it, John taught it, and Paul taught it. Could we possibly need more reason

---

[202] For a more detailed discussion of this passage and call, see Kohler, *Gate Crashers*, 41–55.

to believe that a genuine love for God is the motivation to evangelize? As a final matter for consideration, let's simply examine the basic nature of the Commandments to love God and love others. There were at least two commandments given by Jesus. The first we have already seen several times: to love one another. Another commandment is given after the resurrection and prior to the ascension.

> And Jesus came up and spoke to them, saying, "All authority has been given to Me in heaven and on earth. Go therefore and make disciples of all the nations, baptizing them in the name of the Father and the Son and the Holy Spirit, teaching them to observe all that I commanded you; and lo, I am with you always, even to the end of the age." (Matt 28:18–20)

If we love Jesus, we will obey this commandment by evangelizing and discipling all who respond to the gospel with repentance and faith. What about the commandment to love others? Can this be tied to evangelism also? If we are to love others as we love ourselves, perhaps the questions are, What would you want to happen to you if you were still dead in your trespasses and sins and perishing under the wrath of God? What would you consider a loving act if you were in that situation? Would anything other than being told the gospel of salvation take priority? To what lengths would you desire for those who had the answer to your terrible predicament go to grab your attention and confront you with the message of life and peace with your Creator? Are you willing to go to the same lengths so others may have the opportunity to hear, repent, and believe?

It is hard to conceive of anything being more important than being boldly and lovingly confronted with the gospel if we are under the wrath of God and have only one hope to be reconciled to him. If this is what we would find to be most loving if it were us who were perishing, should we not then love others as we love ourselves?

Michael Green accurately stated,

> Now if you believe that outside of Christ there is no hope, it is impossible to possess an atom of human love

and kindness without being gripped with a great desire to bring men to this one way of salvation. We are not surprised, therefore, to find that concern for the state of the unevangelized was one of the great driving forces behind Christian preaching of the gospel in the early Church.[203]

Has the love in the professing church grown cold today? Why do so few professing Christians share the gospel regularly and meaningfully?

We must be clear on the difference between "discussing our faith with others" and biblical evangelism. Many who claim to evangelize are not evangelizing in a way Jesus, the apostles, or the early church would have recognized as evangelism.[204] I have heard of reports from missionaries who boast of having "spiritual conversations" in the field—a loose definition that seemingly includes saying "God bless you" after someone sneezes since God was mentioned in the conversation!

Jesus warned that as the end drew near, hatred would increase, false prophets would arise and lead people away with their false teaching, and as lawlessness increased, people's love would grow cold. Jesus likewise promised that those who endured until the end would be saved. Jesus reaffirmed that the gospel of the kingdom would be preached in the whole world as a testimony to all the nations, and then the end would come.[205] Some of the prominent false gospels being preached today are the gospel of moralism and a gospel that lacks a need for repentance.[206] Listen carefully to preachers today—many say that all we need to do is believe in Jesus and accept him as Savior. Jesus himself taught that to receive forgiveness of sins, repentance must be preached as a prerequisite.[207] A gospel that lacks a call to repentance is really no gospel at all.

Has your love grown cold? Has modern culture hijacked your definition

---

[203] Green, *Evangelism in the Early Church*, 249.

[204] For a longer discussion of the prominent and dangerous form of false evangelism in which Christians tell nonbelievers the simple phrase, "Jesus loves you!" without further explanation, see the article published on our blog: www. fourthyearministries.com/2014/12/jesus-loves-you.html.

[205] Matt 24:10–14.

[206] For more on the false gospel of moralism, see Kohler, *Gate Crashers*.

[207] Luke 24:45–48.

of love? Or is the love of God such a reality in your life that you cannot help but obey God and live for the praise and glory of his name through the bold, faithful, and loving proclamation of the fullness of the gospel? Like Paul, I pray that the church will be given a genuine understanding of God's amazing love so we too will be controlled by his unfailing love.

To renew and refresh our love, we need only fix our attention on Jesus. He is the key to understanding and experiencing this great love. He is the manifestation, demonstration, and explanation of God's love, for when we were dead in our trespasses and sins—when we were God's enemies—God sent his beloved Son to be the propitiation for our sins. Jesus willingly laid down his life to bear the penalty for our sins so we could be presented before the Father holy, blameless, and pure.[208] Truly, greater love has no one than this![209]

In Christ, we see that God loved his enemies; his people are commanded to do the same. In Christ, we see that Jesus came to seek and save the lost and to lay down his life as a ransom for many; his people are to do the same. In Christ, we see that God magnifies and demonstrates his love; his people are to magnify and declare this glorious love for the praise and honor of his name. In Christ, we see that God first loved us; his people are to lavishly be the first to love others.

God has saved us for a purpose. He intends for us to walk in accordance with his will. The good news is that God has also taken steps to ensure that everyone in the body of Christ is equipped, edified, and empowered to do his or her part. Understanding the purpose and function of the church helps us understand God's design for giving leadership to the body to help all members of the body fulfill their purpose and function.

---

[208] John 10:17–18; Col 1:21–22.
[209] John 15:13.

CHAPTER 7

The Forgotten Officer

*And He gave some as apostles, and some as prophets, and
some as evangelists, and some as pastors and teachers*
—Ephesians 4:11

I take no joy in critiquing the views of my brothers and sisters in Christ. I
have learned far more from the authors I cite in this chapter than they will
learn from me. I am incredibly thankful for the contributions they have
made to the edification of the church through their writing. The following
is offered in the hope of mutual edification and with the hope of exposing
this contemporary theological blind spot.

Evangelist is a word like *church* and *love* that many infuse with
meaning based on their experiences and cultures. Unfortunately, these
preconceptions lead us astray. It is time to take a fresh look at Ephesians
4:11–13 and examine what is really there. It is difficult for people to see
what this part of God's Word reveals. Perhaps the reason is due to some
aspect of spiritual warfare. If my view is accurate, the stakes are high.

When I first started to see the amazing truth Paul wrote to the saints
in Ephesus, God was independently leading my ministry partner Joel
Davidson to see the same thing. We began to discuss it and realized we
were seeing something important; I did what I usually do when I see
something new—I asked other trusted Christians about it. When I asked
about Ephesians 4:11, almost invariably, the discussion that followed was
the same. They would talk a little bit about their views on apostles and
prophets (whether they were for today or not). After that, they would explain
their views on the relationship between pastors and teachers—whether

they view this as two separate ministries/offices (the fivefold view) or if they think they are one and the same ministry/office (the fourfold view). I have a number of relationships with people who have gone to Bible school and seminary, so the conversation on this passage usually revolved around what scholars tend to discuss and debate over.

After hearing their perspectives on the validity of the office and gifts of apostle and prophet for today and getting a clear picture of whether they saw a fivefold or a fourfold ministry, I asked, "What about the evangelists?" It was surprising the first couple of times, but then it became comical as I spoke with more and more Christian friends and leaders. No one had much to say about the evangelists; they had been pretty much forgotten. The thoughts shared were usually fairly superficial, something along the lines of what most people think of—that some itinerant gospel preachers such as Billy Graham and D. L. Moody fit the description of evangelists. Some said the evangelists were basically missionaries who preached the gospel in new places and planted churches.

Not much more to say really; I could tell they hadn't spent much time thinking about this member of the ministry fold—at least, not nearly as much time thinking about them as they had the other members on the list.

This phenomenon is not limited to my acquaintances. In doing research on this forgotten officer or leadership function, I read as widely as I could on church leadership, especially as it pertained to interpretations of Ephesians 4:11 and the implications for the church. Part of the difficulty in discussing this is due to the terminology, which varies from commentator to commentator, used to refer to the members of Ephesians 4:11—functions, officers, gifts, charismatic leaders, elders, bishops, or simply listing each member as its own office (office of apostle, office of prophet, etc.). As a result, the language of offices and officers poses no issue for some when discussing the members of Ephesians 4:11. For others, this type of language imposes barriers because they hold strictly to either a two-office (elders and deacons[210]) or three-office (elders, deacons, pastors) view. Some are comfortable saying that the apostles and the prophets were offices (whether they continue to the present is a separate issue), but the evangelists, pastors, and teachers are not offices but better termed as ministries. Still others are more comfortable calling these the ascension gifts instead of offices or

---

[210] Or "pastors and deacons" in some denominations.

officers. Some will include the pastors (or pastor/teachers in the fourfold ministry view) as rightly included in the discussion of offices or officers but still leave out the evangelists.

And so on it goes. Regardless of our terminology, we must deal with the reality that the risen Christ has given some titled apostles, prophets, evangelists, and pastors and teachers to serve the church in particular ways. Insisting on terminology before assessing what is here will necessarily influence our theological conclusions. If we make decisions about who or what offices and officers exist for the church prior to examining the passage, we are begging the question and must force our interpretive conclusions to fit the context we have established.[211] This is bad interpretive practice; a better practice is to start with what the text actually says and draw whatever conclusions best account for what is there.

Some claim that Ephesians 4:11 does not really include a list of officers but a description of gifted persons who fill a particular function in serving the body of Christ. Frank Viola asserted,

> In short, Ephesians 4:11 doesn't envision a hired clergy,
> a professional ministry, or a special priestcraft. Neither
> are they a special class of Christians. Like Paul's catalog
> of gifts in 1 Corinthians 12:28, Ephesians 4 has in view
> special functions rather than formal positions.[212]

There is much to commend in Viola's view; all Christians should consider important his biblical and historical analysis of the function and form of leadership for the New Testament church. Viola saw many of the same problems I do regarding the pastor-led church model that has elevated a singular leader in a local church fellowship well beyond what was designed by Jesus or described in the New Testament.[213] In contrast to the official and rigid hierarchical forms of church leadership—forms that enhance the so-called clergy/laity divide—Viola stressed what he called a functional mind-set. Here are his own words.

---

[211] "Begging the question" is a logical fallacy that asserts the conclusion in the premises of the argument.

[212] Viola, *Reimagining Church*, 292.

[213] See also, Viola and Barna, *Pagan Christianity?* chapter 5.

Leadership in the New Testament places a high premium on the unique gifting, spiritual maturity, and sacrificial service of each member. It lays stress on functions, not offices. It emphasizes tasks rather than titles. Its main concern lies in activities like pastor-*ing*, elder-*ing*, prophesy-*ing*, oversee-*ing*, apostle-*ing*, etc.

To frame it another way, positional thinking is hung up on nouns, while functional thinking stresses verbs.[214]

Of course, the full idea of leadership expressed in the New Testament uses both nouns and verbs. To stress one over the other can lead to improper conclusions and is the product of another interpretive fallacy, which sets a false dichotomy before us in saying that the New Testament either stresses verbs or nouns. The reality is not either but both. By diminishing the Bible's use of nouns for particular leadership roles (whether we call them offices or functions is arguing semantics), Viola was led to interpret the list of nouns in Ephesians 4:11 inaccurately.

You will notice that evangelists do not make his list of functions either. It may be because evangelist-*ing* or evangelism-*ing* does nothing to clarify their function for the church or because it seems obvious that evangelize-*ing* is the function of evangelists, namely, sharing the gospel with the lost as their primary function, pushing evangelists into a category of leadership that is not necessarily in the church but outside it. As such, evangelist-*ing* seems to be a function best performed in the parachurch ministry as is most commonly experienced in our culture. (I will discuss this inaccurate understanding in greater detail in chapter 8.)

Viola made an excellent observation regarding the functional aspect of the leadership roles in Ephesians 4.

Their chief task is to nurture the believing community into responsible roles. Their success is rooted in their ability to

---

[214] Viola, *Reimagining Church*, 154. Viola repeats this idea later, saying, "in other words, New Testament leadership can best be understood in terms of *verbs* rather than *nouns*" (ibid., 177, italics in original).

empower and mobilize God's people for the work of the
ministry. In this way, the Ephesians 4 gifts equip the body
to fulfill God's eternal purpose.[215]

While he has done a commendable job of identifying the functional
aspect of these leadership roles, he made a clear interpretive error when
he asserted, "These ascension gifts are not offices. Nor are they formal
positions. The Greek has no definite article connected with these terms."[216]

This is false; the Greek does have definite articles connected with the
terms in Ephesians 4:11. His argument lacks foundation in the reality of
what is in the text. The New Testament emphasizes both nouns and verbs
in relationship to leadership roles and functions. We cannot eliminate the
nouns because some have unduly elevated these functions to unhealthy
positions of leadership that lord their authority over the body instead of
lovingly using their gifts to serve and edify.[217]

Similarly, we cannot simply explain away these positions and assert
they were "unofficial" or "informal" as Viola attempted to do since we
have clear indication from the Scriptures that Paul could call for the elders
of a city and expect them to show up.[218] If the elders were an informal,
unofficial group, how could Paul send for them and expect them to come?
Who was supposed to respond to this invitation if not those who were
formally and officially filling this office or function in the local church?
Likewise, the terminology of "the apostles" is not a vague term that refers
to some indistinct or unofficial segment of the body of Christ. The apostles

---

[215] Ibid., 292.

[216] Ibid.

[217] Viola's argument for these functions serving informally and unofficially is largely
based on Jesus' teaching on leadership in places such as Mark 10:42–45. Viola
also cited works relating to the doctrine of the Trinity in explaining how
relationships and authority ought to function properly. For those interested
in a discussion of the Trinitarian nature of God that recognizes authority and
functional subordination (not to be confused with ontological subordination,
which is heretical) and a detailed biblical case that authority can be exercised
lovingly and officially without "lording" it over those who are in submission, are
encouraged to read Ware, *Father, Son, & Holy Spirit*, and Grudem, *Systematic
Theology*, chapter 14.

[218] E.g., Acts 20:17–18.

were clearly recognized as official; unofficial apostles were regarded as false apostles.

Despite this interpretive error, Viola made many important and accurate observations regarding leadership in the New Testament, and his writings are worth a careful and thoughtful read. He is correct that the modern fascination with elevating the senior or lead pastor above the rest of the plurality of leadership in the local fellowship is particularly unhealthy for the pastor and the body. However, we need not sacrifice the position to maintain the function. We can recognize both since the Scriptures affirm both.[219] Gordon Fee offered a good summary: "The leaders are not 'over' the church, but are addressed 'alongside of' the church, as a *distinguishable* part of the whole, but as *part of the whole*, not above or outside it."[220]

T. David Gordon made the following observations on the relationship between Ephesians 4:11 and 4:12.

> Briefly, the sentence is constructed in this way. There is a main verb (*edōken*) followed by several direct objects (each introduced by the article *tous*). The purpose of Christ's giving these officers to the Church is described in the three purpose clauses (introduced by the telic prepositions *pros* and *eis*), and the extent or degree of the purpose clauses is explicated by the following *mechri*.[221]

Notice how Gordon rightly identified that Ephesians 4:11 listed officers given to the church by Christ whose purpose and function is described in the following verse(s). Notice also that he rightly included that each of these officers were introduced in the Greek by the definite article (which Viola denied). Gordon's analysis of this passage continued immediately with his translation of Ephesians 4:11–13.

---

[219] See also Carson's discussion of a similar example of an unwarranted semantic disjunction in regard to authority in *Exegetical Fallacies*, 55–57.

[220] As cited by Selby, "Bishops, Elders, and Deacons," 82, from Fee, *Paul's Letter to the Philippians*, 67, emphasis in original.

[221] Gordon, "'Equipping' Ministry in Ephesians 4?" 71.

> He gave some to be apostles, some prophets, some pastors
> and teachers; for the purpose of (their) perfecting the
> saints, doing the ministry, and edifying the body of
> Christ, to the extent that all would attain the unity of
> the faith and knowledge of God's Son, mature humanity,
> and the measure of the stature of the fullness of Christ.[222]

Keep in mind that this is a peer-reviewed article published in a leading theology journal. Did you notice anything missing? Reread the translation of Ephesians 4:11–13. What happened to the evangelists? They have simply disappeared. Maybe it was a typo. However, this is not an isolated case.

In an article entitled "The Pastor an Evangelist" in *Baker's Handbook of Practical Theology,* Harold J. Ockenga moved through five main sections,[223] and in the final section, he wrote,

> The New Testament emphasizes the fact that there are
> different callings and ministries and offices. The Holy
> Spirit bestows upon different individuals different gifts
> and callings for the good of the church. There are some
> apostles, some prophets, some teachers and pastors, some
> with gifts of healings, some with the ability to help, some
> with ability to govern, etc.[224]

Again, what happened to the evangelists?

In the list from Ephesians 4:11, we have all present but the evangelists again! You may say, "Well, the article is titled 'The Pastor an Evangelist,' so clearly the author is intending these two to be equated." However, the article never made such a claim. Similarly, the above quote falls directly under the heading "The Pastor as Apostle," yet *apostle* is listed clearly and distinctly from pastors in the quote. The evangelists are once again forgotten and excluded.

It doesn't stop there. Norman Geisler, one of my favorite theologians,

---

[222] Ibid.

[223] They are 1. The Pastor as Herald, 2. The Pastor as Ambassador, 3. The Pastor as Messenger, 4. The Pastor as Missionary, and 5. The Pastor as Apostle.

[224] Ockenga, "The Pastor an Evangelist," 170.

has an excellent and thorough treatment of the church in his *Systematic Theology*. Some of the observations he makes regarding the importance of the leaders listed in Ephesians 4:11 are as follows. First, Geisler noted, "Ephesians 4:8–11 declares that the church is dependent on the functioning gifts of her various members, which were given only after [the resurrection and ascension of Christ]."[225] He continued,

> According to Ephesians 4:11–12, the gifts God gave to operate His church included "apostles; and some prophets; and some, evangelists; and some, pastors and teachers; for the perfecting of the saints, for the work of the ministry, for the edifying of the body of Christ" (KJV). Since the body cannot exist without the gifts by which it is sustained, it follows that the church could not exist until after these gifts were given.[226]

Here, Geisler made an important observation that the gifts mentioned in Ephesians 4:11 were necessary for sustaining the church. He repeated this powerful and important point in his discussion reiterating that the gifts listed in Ephesians 4:11–12 were needed to operate the church.[227]

Geisler also made an important contrast with the apostles and prophets—who were a universal gift to the church in their foundational capacity—and the gifts of evangelists and pastors: "On the other hand, pastors and evangelists were/are God's gifts to the *local* church."[228] This makes perfect sense considering Geisler's understanding of the function of each local church stated just a few pages earlier, *"edification is the internal mission of the church, and evangelism is the external mission."*[229] To fulfill these internal and external missions, each local church has the necessary government (as all church government is local church government in Geisler's analysis[230]), which explains why Christ would give the necessary

---

[225] Geisler, *Systematic Theology*, 4:24.

[226] Ibid., 4:25–26.

[227] Ibid., 4:56.

[228] Ibid., 4:106, italics in original.

[229] Ibid., 4:95, italics in original.

[230] Ibid., 4:96.

gifts of evangelists and pastors and teachers for the equipping of the saints in any particular place to fulfill their mission as a local body.

It is important at this point to recognize that Geisler distinguished between the gifts Christ gave and the offices recognized in the local church government. The gifts for the church governance are listed in Ephesians 4:11, whereas the offices recognized are that of elder and deacon.[231] According to Geisler, the gifts of apostle and prophet are noncontinuing gifts in regard to the persons filling them but continue to be foundational and authoritative for the church today through the apostolic writings—the New Testament.[232] In contrast, the gifts of evangelists and pastor/teachers are abiding gifts,[233] which means they have endured to the present. These abiding gifts of evangelists and pastor/teachers are gifts of persons in leadership for the local church.

To this point, Geisler did a much better job of accurately handling the text before us and identifying the important points than those who have simply erased the evangelists from the list. However, in his discussion of the relationship between the office of elder and the gifts in Ephesians 4, Geisler did not discuss evangelists or prophets. Since the prophets were not an enduring gift in his view, it makes sense they would be excluded from his discussion. However, to leave out evangelists and discuss only the relationship between elders and pastors is perplexing.[234]

Geisler returned to the topic of evangelists before concluding his material on the church when discussing spiritual gifts. Unfortunately, Geisler made the error of equating the gift of evangelists (people) with the spiritual gift of evangelism for much of his discussion.[235] While this error is common, it is nonetheless an error. If we hold to the inspiration of the Scriptures down to the very words themselves (as I know Geisler in fact does[236]), we cannot simply equate two different words as if they were the same; Evangelists ≠ evangelism. The assertion by even capable theologians does not make it so.

---

[231] Ibid., 4:106.

[232] For a fuller discussion, see ibid., 4:91–93, 101–2, 105–6, 117–18, 125, 725–26.

[233] Geisler holds to the fourfold ministry model that combines pastors and teachers into one grouping; see ibid., 4:201.

[234] Ibid., 4:117–122. The absence of discussion concerning teachers is explained by Geisler's fourfold ministry view of Eph 4:11.

[235] For a more detailed discussion of this error, see Kohler, *Gate Crashers*, 122–47.

[236] Geisler gives a powerful, thorough, and convincing case for the verbal, plenary inspiration of the Bible in Geisler, *Systematic Theology*, 1:229–43.

This error of asserting that evangelists are those gifted with the spiritual gift of evangelism becomes even more destructive when trying to define the abiding gift of evangelists as revealed in the Scriptures because our assertion then obscures what is plainly stated in God's Word.[237] By improperly defining the scope of the ongoing work of the evangelists, Geisler then is free to mistakenly separate them from pastors and teachers in their enduring role in the local church. However, there is no textual or grammatical reason to separate any of the gifts listed in Ephesians 4:11 from the description of their ministry and the purpose for them stated in 4:12. Commentators who explain the evangelists away as noncontinuing ministries—akin to the apostles and prophets—can justify separating out pastors and teachers as those who are called to equip the saints and edify the body in the present,[238] but Geisler's model does not allow for this possibility. Sadly, his erroneous presupposition that evangelists equal those with the spiritual gift of evangelism has caused him to ignore the evangelists in his final assessment of local church governance.

This is tragic. Remember that Geisler began with strong and accurate assertions that the gifts in Ephesians 4:11 were necessary for the continuing of the church, that evangelists were an abiding gift, and that they were for the local church. Look at how the simple error of defining evangelists as those with the spiritual gift of evangelism caused him to forget the evangelists by the time he concluded his discussion on the gifts.

> The internal purpose of the local church is edification so that its members can do the work of the ministry; evangelism is also a prime mission. ... Nonetheless, as Paul indicated, the gift(s) of pastor and teacher still exist today and are to be used for "edifying of the body of Christ: Till we all come to the unity of the faith, and of the knowledge of the Son of God, to a perfect man, to the measure of the stature of the fullness of Christ" (Eph. 4:12–13 NKJV).[239]

---

[237] Ibid., 4:202. This and other errors, will be discussed in greater detail in chapter 8.

[238] This error will also be covered in more detail in chapter 8.

[239] Geisler, *Systematic Theology*, 4:213.

Geisler has not lost focus on the prime mission of the church. He has, however, lost an important, abiding, and necessary gift that contributes to fulfilling the mission of the church and the growth of the body to the fullness of Christ. By his own statements, this is no small loss. The effects are felt in disruptions to unity, knowledge of Jesus, the edification of the body, and our growth together into the fullness of what God has designed. Geisler rightly observed that evangelists were necessary to the proper functioning of the church and that they were abiding gifts to the local body. This means that forgetting them will cause us to lose something essential to the life and health of the local body.

Another esteemed theologian followed a similar course. In discussing church officers, Wayne Grudem listed four: apostles, elders, deacons, and others.[240] The "others" is a catchall that allows for officers such as treasurers, trustees, paid staff, etc. What is most interesting for the present discussion is the breadth of Grudem's office of elder, which he defines to include pastors, overseers, and bishops. This is not uncommon.[241] What is perplexing is the ease with which evangelists are once again left out of this conversation with no explanation.

Here are some examples.

> Elders are also called "pastors" or "bishops" or "overseers" in the New Testament. The least commonly used word (at least in the noun form) is *pastor* (Gk. *poimēn*). It may be surprising to us to find that this word, which has become so common in English, only occurs once in the New Testament when speaking about a church officer. In Ephesians 4:11, Paul writes, "And his gifts were that some should be apostles, some prophets, some evangelists, some *pastors* and teachers."[242]

Grudem explained why he held to the fourfold ministry view, but he gave no mention as to why we could pluck pastors from this list of officers

---

[240] Grudem, *Systematic Theology*, 905–20.

[241] See, e.g., Merkle, *40 Questions About Elders and Deacons*, 54–58. More on this in chapter 8.

[242] Grudem, *Systematic Theology*, 913, italics in original.

and equate them with elders while neglecting the others. Again, Grudem asserted, "In Ephesians 4:11, elders are referred to as 'pastor-teachers' (or, on an alternative translation, pastors who are viewed as quite closely united to teachers)."[243] While I do not disagree with Grudem's identification of pastors as elders, I do raise the question as to what interpretive warrant we have for simply plucking people out of the list in Ephesians 4:11 and excluding others.

George W. Knight III argued persuasively for the proper inclusion of all the members of Ephesians 4:11 in the office of elder. Unlike many other commentators who simply excluded or forgot about the evangelists, Knight made a case for including each officer listed in Ephesians 4:11 based on exegetical reasoning.

> The officers in the church at Ephesus are referred to as elders or bishops in Acts 20:17, 28 and 1 Timothy 3:1 and 5:17 and as evangelists and pastors and teachers in Ephesians 4:11. Both because of what we have seen in the preceding statements, that is apostles are fellow elders, and prophets and teachers perform the action of presbytery by laying on hands, and because Acts, 1 Timothy, and Ephesians refer to the same church and the same officers, we may properly infer as a good and necessary consequence that evangelists and pastors and teachers are elders. Certainly the Ephesians passage regards them as leaders who equip the church, a task recognized elsewhere as the particular responsibility of elders (cf. among others, Acts 20:28; 1 Tim 3:4, 5 and 5:17).[244]

Though Knight made an etymologically based interpretive error[245] in defining the precise nature of the ministry of the evangelists in the midst of his comments on the officers listed in Ephesians 4:11, he made important observations as well.

---

[243] Ibid., 915.

[244] Knight, "Two Offices," 4.

[245] See the discussion of the common "root fallacy" in Carson, *Exegetical Fallacies*, 28–33, where Carson gave an excellent discussion and several examples—my

> The first two groups, apostles and prophets, are the extraordinary and non-repeatable foundation offices, as we have shown earlier. … In view of the fact that the gift of proclaiming the gospel and planting churches is necessary in the church until the end of the age, this ministry [of evangelists] is permanent and not confined to the apostolic period. And because evangelists in Ephesians 4:11 are in the list of these offices which are distinguished from the saints or believers in general (Eph 4:12), we may properly regard them as a specialized manifestation of that office whose task is elsewhere described in similar terms to those used here, that of edifying and equipping the saints, namely, the office of elder (Eph 4:11. 12).[246]

Knight was right to include evangelists in the discussion of the office of elder. He has rightly concluded that the ministry of the evangelists was permanent and tied to edifying and equipping the saints. Unfortunately, his etymological error caused him to inaccurately portray the scope of the ministry of the evangelists.

After arguing for the inclusion of evangelists among the elders in the local church, Knight wrote, "Evangelists are gaining lost sheep, not caring for saved and gathered ones. So the apostle has placed that aspect of the teaching eldership, evangelists, in a separate category and recognizes that some have special gifts for that task."[247] I will deal with this interpretive error in more detail in chapter 8, but for the present discussion, I will

---

favorite of which is the poverty of attempting to derive the meaning of "butterfly" from "butter" and "fly" or "pineapple" from "pine" and "apple." Likewise, Geisler commented that "etymology is not the key to the meaning of a term. … The fact that the word *board* originally meant a wooden plank is not helpful in determining its meaning in the term 'Chairman of the Board'" (Geisler, *Systematic Theology*, 1:165). To assume, then, that evangelists only proclaim the gospel to the lost because the term contains the root *euangel* is erroneous especially when this interpretation contradicts the explicit revelation of God's Word as to the purpose of Christ giving evangelists in Eph 4:12. As if the gospel were for nonbelievers only!

[246] Knight, "Two Offices," 9.
[247] Ibid., 11.

simply affirm what Carson so accurately stated: "Specification of the meaning of a word on the sole basis of etymology can never be more than an educated guess."[248]

Despite this particular error, Knight's exegetical insights demonstrate that the casual disregard some commentators use for excluding evangelists from the discussion of local church governance is inappropriate. We cannot simply dismiss the evangelists with a wave of the hand.

If theologians and commentators wish to eliminate this officer from the discussion of elders and the continuing governance in and of the local church, we should at least see some exegetical warrant for their interpretive conclusions. However, instead of providing careful exegetical reasoning, the evangelists are often simply forgotten when discussing the church through theological sleight of hand: now you see me, now you don't.

When the evangelist is discussed, interpretive errors, assumptions, and assertions tend to dominate the discussion and mingle much error amid what good is presented. For example, Grudem made the common error of equating evangelists and the spiritual gift of evangelism.

> Among those who possess the gift of evangelism, some will be good at personal evangelism within a neighborhood, others at evangelism through writing of tracts and Christian literature, and others at evangelism through large campaigns and public meetings. Still others will be good at evangelism through radio and television. Not all of these evangelistic gifts are the same, even though they fall under the broad category of "evangelism."[249]

Grudem's analysis of the "spiritual gift of evangelism" was based entirely on his own authority, experience, and assertions; there is no biblical foundation for any of his statements because the "spiritual gift" of evangelism is nowhere mentioned in the Bible.[250] Grudem asserted his opinion on the proper interpretation of Ephesians 4:11 in this way: "This list gives four kinds of persons in terms of offices or functions, not, strictly speaking,

---

[248] Carson, *Exegetical Fallacies*, 33.

[249] Grudem, *Systematic Theology*, 1021.

[250] For more detailed discussion of this reality, see Kohler, *Gate Crashers*, 122–47.

four gifts. For three of the functions on the list, the corresponding gifts would be prophecy, evangelism, and teaching."[251] These observations are not exegetically based but are merely the assertions of the commentator. Prophecy and teaching are recognized as spiritual gifts in the Bible while evangelism is not.[252] In fact, the ministry of reconciliation (evangelism) is a ministry that every Christian is given and expected to be equipped to participate in.[253]

Grudem went further when he wrote,

> Some lists name only the gifts themselves (such as 1 Cor. 12:8–10), while other lists name only the people who possess those gifts (such as Eph. 4:11 or 1 Peter 4:11). ... Similarly, the New Testament does not clearly indicate that prophets or evangelists were established in any formally recognized offices in the early church, and the word "prophet" probably just refers to one who prophesied regularly and with evident blessing in the church. "Evangelist" could similarly refer to those who regularly functioned effectively in the work of evangelism.[254]

Do you see the language that indicates by Grudem's own assessment that these conclusions are shaky at best? They are based solely on Grudem's "probably" and "could be" assertions.

Unfortunately and uncharacteristically, the biblical evidence is not in Grudem's favor here. The identification of Philip as "the evangelist" in Caesarea in Acts 21:8 is strong evidence that the local church did recognize this office. Philip was not simply *an* evangelist who happened to live there; he was *the* evangelist and had been residing in Caesarea for the twenty years that had passed since he had arrived there in Acts 8:40. Similarly, Acts 13:1 could very soundly be interpreted as having prophets and teachers as official officers in the church at Antioch. The point is that even excellent theologians such as Grudem have been uncharacteristically

---

[251] Grudem, *Systematic Theology*, 1020n8.

[252] Rom 12:6–8; 1 Cor 12:10; 1 Pet 4:11.

[253] 2 Cor 5:17–21.

[254] Grudem, *Systematic Theology*, 1021n9.

shallow in their analysis of the biblical data regarding the office or gift of evangelist. It may be "evident" to Grudem that those listed in Ephesians 4:11 have gifts corresponding to the office, but there is no biblical warrant beyond the assertion of its being "evident" without adequately dealing with alternative interpretations and views.[255]

The reality cannot be quickly dismissed; commentary on the biblical gift of evangelists from the risen Lord Jesus for the edification of his church is shallow and filled with errors. In some cases, the gift is completely forgotten and excluded; in other cases, the evangelists are explained away or neglected due to improper exegetical handling and the assertions of the commentator. Whether forgotten or neglected, the result is the same—evangelists are excluded from their proper place in their leadership roles for the church as they were given by Jesus, which will hinder the church from attaining unity of the faith, knowledge of the Son of God, maturity, and the measure of the stature that belongs to the fullness of Christ according to Ephesians 4:13.

Under the inspiration of the Holy Spirit, the apostle Paul was led to include evangelists among the ascension gifts mentioned in Ephesians 4:11 that Jesus gave to his church. His understanding and the understanding of the early church of the function of this important role led to vastly different activities throughout the body than our redefined notions do. Though Millard Erickson made some of the same errors as other commentators regarding the role of evangelists, he rightly agreed with the conclusions of Geisler and Grudem that one of the major purposes of the church (the whole body, every member) was to evangelize.

> The one topic emphasized in both accounts of Jesus' last words to his disciples is evangelism. … This was the final point Jesus made to his disciples. It appears that he regarded evangelism as the very reason for their being. … If the disciples truly loved their Lord, they would carry out his call to evangelize. It was not an optional matter for them.[256]

---

[255] For more on this type of interpretive fallacy, see Carson, *Exegetical Fallacies*, 122.
[256] Erickson, *Christian Theology*, 1061.

Understanding their purpose to evangelize (locally, by planting churches, and continuing in world missions), Erickson stated, "If [a local church] does not [evangelize], it will become spiritually ill, for it will be attempting to function in a way its Lord never intended."[257] Many local churches today function as if evangelism were optional or treat it as simply one ministry among many. No wonder they are spiritually ill.

Despite observing the necessary function of the church to evangelize, Erickson likewise lost sight of the evangelists when he described the church's need to disciple.

> The church also edifies its members through instruction or teaching. This is part of the broad task of discipling. One of Jesus' commands in the Great Commission was to teach converts "to obey everything I have commanded you" (Matt 28:20). To this end, one of God's gifts to the churches is "pastors and teachers" (Eph 4:11) to prepare and equip the people of God for service.[258]

Again I ask, what about evangelists? Were they not also given for this task according to Ephesians 4:11–12? Would they not help in this regard of world evangelization and discipleship in obeying all Christ's commands (including the command to proclaim the gospel to every creature)?

We have inherited a church culture that does not rightly understand, appreciate, value, or recognize evangelists in the local church. At best, we recognize the ministry of evangelists as a parachurch ministry. As a result, we have separated evangelists from their biblical position and have even become blind to what is plainly stated in the Scriptures regarding this office and function of church leaders. We have nullified the Word of God with our human traditions. We should not be surprised to find a largely immature body constantly tossed here and there by waves and winds of doctrine. We are lacking an important officer whose job is to help us speak the truth in love, which is critical for us growing up in all aspects into Christ.[259]

---

[257] Ibid., 1063.

[258] Ibid., 1064–65.

[259] Eph 4:14–15.

Over time, the effects have become obvious. Erickson noted, "In biblical times the church gathered for worship and instruction. Then it went out to evangelize."[260] Today, most Christians gather to worship, receive instruction ... then disperse to get on with the rest of their day. This modern response bears more resemblance to the Israelites worshiping the golden calf than the activities of the early church.[261]

As soon as our local church recognized the proper biblical role of the evangelist in the church, this was the first change that happened. It was not because of reading widely on the opinions of what Christians should do but a result of keeping the proper focus that the church exists to worship God, to be edified and built up, and to spread the glorious gospel to the ends of the earth. Our evangelist worked tirelessly to bring as many of those who gathered for worship through song, word, and sacrament to continue worshiping God together by taking the gospel to our community together as we dismissed.

Everett Ferguson affirmed that the work of the church included evangelization. He claimed that when this activity stopped, the church died. For Ferguson, the true church was a church that preached the gospel, and he did not mean just the pastors and staff members.[262] As a result, "When the church fails to do the work of Christ, it becomes the corpse instead of the body of Christ."[263]

What has happened? Why did the early church take this task so seriously—even at risk to their well-being—while many today in the professing church view evangelism as some optional ministry to be engaged in only by those who are specially gifted for that purpose? This is a result of our failure to properly recognize and value Christ's gift of evangelists as revealed in the Scriptures.

Green accurately observed that "the apostolic Church were quite clear that God's gift of his Spirit was intended not to make them comfortable but to make them witnesses."[264] In accordance with this, Christ gave leadership gifts to his body to fulfill this purpose. As a result of embracing

---

[260] Erickson, *Christian Theology*, 1066.

[261] Exod 32:1–6; 1 Cor 10:6–14.

[262] See Ferguson, *The Church of Christ*, 284–86.

[263] Ibid., 284.

[264] Green, *Evangelism in the Early Church*, 72.

the apostolic foundation for the role of leadership and body, those initiated into the faith through baptism after positively responding to the gospel had certain expectations on their lives.

> And the baptismal life not only involved holy living and Christian love, but also worship and fellowship, witness and instruction. The first converts continued in the apostles' doctrine and fellowship, the breaking of bread and the prayers: and with one accord they bore their testimony to Jesus.[265]

Many churches are good at emphasizing doctrine, fellowship, and prayer but neglect unified witness of Christ because pastors and teachers, not evangelists, dominate their leadership structures. The body reflects the gap in leadership because the leadership is designed to eliminate the gap when it is fully represented and functioning properly.

I could cite many more examples, but I have made my point. After examining the text, our best option is to understand that all the members listed in Ephesians 4:11 are rightly included under the broad category of "elders"—officially, that is their office. However, it is superficial to then say all these categories of elders are the same; they are not. Apostles, prophets, evangelists, and pastors and teachers are all distinctions with significance and are worthy of being recognized as their own category of elder. In this way, it is not inaccurate or contrary to the Scriptures to affirm that Peter was an apostle, that Agabus was a prophet, and that Philip was an evangelist, that each of these men were elders, and that their functions were not eldering in general but overseeing in a very specialized way tied to their unique category of elder.

The members listed in Ephesians 4:11 are explicitly given by Jesus: *"And He [the risen Christ] gave some* as apostles, and some as prophets, and some as evangelists, and some as pastors and teachers" (Eph 4:11, italics added). No one is ever told to aspire to the office of apostle, prophet, evangelist, or pastor/teacher[266] even though we are told, "It is a trustworthy statement:

---

[265] Ibid., 156.

[266] Passages such as Heb 5:12 and Jas 3:1 indicate that the body in general ought to be producing "teachers," but on the fourfold view (which I take) these teachers

if any man aspires to the office of overseer, it is a fine work he desires to do" (1 Tim 3:1). The members of Ephesians 4:11 are given by Christ for the equipping of the saints and for the growth of the body to maturity according to Ephesians 4:12–16. As the body grows to maturity, we would expect that nonapostles, nonprophets, nonevangelists, and nonpastors/teachers would be able to grow to positions of leadership and oversight for the benefit of the body as elders or deacons. If they become elders, one of the requirements is that they are able to teach,[267] which means they will fill a role as teachers (by word and deed) in the body in addition to the other elders (that is, the terminology of "teachers" applies equally to the evangelist-elder, pastor/teacher-elder, and elder-elder).[268]

However, a Christian who grows to maturity and eventually fills the office of overseer/elder is not the same as an apostle, prophet, evangelist, or pastor/teacher who was given by Christ by special appointment and calling. By maintaining these distinctions, we affirm the office of elder while understanding that the particular categories of elder (whether apostle, prophet, evangelist, pastor/teacher) are distinctions with significance from those who are elders as a result of the regular Christian maturity process. Neither should be considered better or more important than the other, but there is a difference in the language Scripture uses in describing them.

I believe it is best to affirm that the terminology of *office* and *officers* is appropriate when discussing the members of Ephesians 4:11. The titles are rightly understood as an office (albeit a subcategory of the broader office of elder/overseer) that describes the function of the particular officers in their oversight of the body of Christ. There are qualifications and expectations of elders that apply to all in this office whatever subcategory they fill.

There are also different expectations and differing functions of the subcategories that must be preserved and properly recognized for the edification of the body. While all elders should mutually submit to each other in the local church, there is a distinction of function that warrants its own title and is rightly described as an office in its own right. To say that apostles are elders, evangelists are elders, and pastors are elders does

---

are different from the pastor/teachers in Ephesians 4:11. These teachers are built by spiritual maturity and not necessarily through spiritual gifting.

[267] Which is different from being gifted to teach.

[268] 1 Cor 12:28; Heb 5:12; Jas 3:1; 1 Tim 3:2; 2 Tim 2:2, 24; Titus 1:9; 1 Pet 5:1–3.

not mean that we must say apostles, evangelists, and pastors are the same; they are not.

My suggestion, based on a careful examination of what the text actually says, is that the apostles, prophets, evangelists, and pastor/teachers are all officers in the office of elder. These are shorthand titles with distinction that help the church differentiate between apostle-elders, prophet-elders, evangelist-elders, pastor/teacher-elders, and elder-elders.

Understanding the problem, we will turn our attention to an analysis of the popular but inadequate views regarding the gift of evangelists before submitting an alternative interpretation that I present to the church as a better way of understanding the gift of evangelists as revealed through the Scriptures. To forget or redefine the office of elder in regard to the function of the evangelists is a severe error that must be addressed for the edification of the church, the evangelization of the world, and the glory of our God.

Aaron—A Testimony

(Aaron is a research assistant and guest lecturer. He personally shares the gospel with hundreds to thousands of individuals each year.)

I grew up going to church: I was taught to read the Bible, pray, and seek to know God. But by the time I was almost thirty, I had never shared the gospel of Jesus Christ with anyone—at least not as I do now. I think I knew the gospel intellectually and could answer some questions about who God is, who man is, and what Jesus Christ did for man, but I was never equipped to explain the truth of the gospel in a reasonable, logical, and orderly way.

Furthermore, it was never my goal to speak to others about the truth of the gospel. My goal was to live in a way that reflected my understanding and belief of the gospel. I failed at this because I didn't fully understand the gospel myself and because I was still living to please myself most of the time. I had a very self-centered view of God and his redemptive work through his Son.

I had been a professing Christian who sought mostly to receive from Christ and sought to serve Christ only with my moral acts. I opened doors for others, I smiled at others, I prayed for others, I was involved in social activities that helped provide things for others, and I worshiped God with others. None of these acts are bad, but though I often had the opportunity to verbally share the message I believed, I never thought I should or was equipped to be that bold. I believed my lifestyle was the only message I needed.

I never once simply opened my mouth to lovingly share with others the truth I believed saved me, changed me, and redeemed me. I would share portions of the gospel here and there, but never the complete message. My focus had become doing nice things for others instead of verbally sharing the gospel in love—as if these things were mutually exclusive. I trusted in my moments of morality to change people instead of the message Christians were commanded to share, the message Christians have died for and continue to die for, the message that is the power of God unto salvation for all those who believe.

I had often thought, even at age thirty, potentially halfway through life, that God would eventually give me the necessary knowledge and wisdom and cause me to obey his call to boldly proclaim the gospel. As I saw it, my part was to simply wait for God to do all these things. In the last few years, God has done this but in a way I was not expecting: he used others to push me from the state of waiting to actual obedience.

I see now that while I was waiting on God, he was waiting on me to obey what he already revealed for me to do in his Word. Though I should diligently prepare to know God more and to read, understand, and apply what God teaches through his Word, I have learned not only to be obedient but also to rely on the working of the Holy Spirit through me because the Holy Spirit was always wholly prepared to accomplish what he wanted.

I have currently been in fellowship in a local church under the direction of an evangelist and a pastor for four years. As a result, the focus of my life has become less about doing all the moral things and not doing all the immoral things (though I am always seeking to deny my flesh and be conformed to the image of Christ more and more) and more about obedience to Christ. We have been given a commission as Christians—go and make disciples of all nations, baptizing them in the name of the Father, the Son, and the Holy Spirit and teaching them to obey all that Jesus commands. As a local church, we have focused on becoming equipped to continue the ministry of reconciliation through the sharing of the gospel and growing in maturity in Christ and unity together as we speak the truth in love.

We have studied the Bible together seeking a true understanding of who God is. We have practiced presenting the gospel message to others in a clear, concise, caring, and loving way. We have practiced making sure we leave no part of the gospel of Christ out of our message by presenting the whole gospel; sharing who God revealed himself to be in the Scriptures and who man is revealed to be; explaining how we have rebelled against God; and showing who Jesus Christ is and how he came to do the will of his Father, dying for the sins of the world, and being raised to life and exalted to the right hand of God the Father. We have learned to rely on this message and the Holy Spirit to use us in our everyday lives. Beyond this, we also plan to testify about reconciliation to God through Christ to those in our community.

For the last four years, we have gone out to the streets at least once a week to share this message together. We do this out of loving obedience to our Father, who has called us to be ambassadors for Christ. We do this because we care for others and believe in the judgment to come. Our evangelist has led all these outreach activities and much of our training. Without our evangelist, we might have fizzled out (or never fizzled in the first place) as many other groups did prior to the evangelist being part of the leadership team (that is, when the local church was under the pastor-only model of leadership).

Without our evangelist, we would have shared this important message less, we would be less equipped to share the truth, and we would be overtaken with nervousness instead of preparedness and led by the Holy Spirit. Our evangelist is called by God to lead in this manner, and God has used him to lead and equip our church to be ambassadors for Christ. He is a gift to our local church body.

The transition in my life described above was not easy, however. When our evangelist prepared and led many in our church to boldly preach the gospel to strangers and friends, I wanted no part of it. I felt the message and the tack were forced, too bold, and would just make people (including me) uncomfortable. But as we studied Scripture, as we read about the gospel that Jesus, John the Baptist, the apostle Paul, the prophets in the Old Testament, and countless other faithful and obedient followers of Christ repeatedly proclaimed, I realized my thoughts were incorrect. The gospel was proclaimed unabashedly and everywhere with boldness and with reliance on God to do the actual work of salvation, of change. I was forced to confront my perception of how I thought things should be done and to be led by an evangelist who did so in accordance with the Bible.

During this tough transition, I evaluated what I thought it meant to be a Christian, to be a child of God. Ultimately, I was asking myself, asking God, if I even was a child of God. I had to evaluate the fruit being produced. I was specifically confronted by what I read in Matthew 7:21–23.

> Not everyone who says to Me, "Lord, Lord," will enter the kingdom of heaven, but he who does the will of My Father who is in heaven will enter. Many will say to Me on that day, "Lord, Lord, did we not prophesy in Your name, and in Your name cast out demons, and in Your name perform many miracles?" And then I will declare to them, "I never knew you; depart from Me, you who practice lawlessness."

Had I been doing the will of the Father? Had I been seeking to glorify God's name through my obedience as a professed ambassador for Christ—one who represented his message, the gospel, just as Christians were commissioned? As I wrestled with and sought God about the truth of Scripture, I don't think it was too important for me to dwell on whether I was a regenerated Christian but to be thankful for the discipline brought to me by God and seek to be obedient to his commands. I am so thankful God's discipline, though painful, brought forth repentance in me. I am so thankful God is working in his church—he used a pastor and teacher in our body to show me the truth of Scripture and how it should be applied in my life. God also used an evangelist to lead me to apply the truth we received.

The opportunity to be led to obedience in the bold proclamation of the gospel (in planned evangelism trips and in everyday life), one-on-one conversations, and endless giving of gospel tracts has removed my focus from myself and how I can be a "better Christian." It has helped me instead to keep my eyes on Jesus Christ, the author and perfecter of my faith, and to seek to glorify God through obedience to the call he has given those who are his.

The focus of our entire church life is obedience to Christ.

CHAPTER 8

Inadequate Views

But you, be sober in all things, endure hardship, do the
work of an evangelist, fulfill your ministry.
—2 Timothy 4:5

Before presenting what I believe to be the best understanding of the work
and role of evangelists in the church as given by Jesus, I first take note of
the options. After we examine the common interpretations in light of the
biblical testimony, we will see they are lacking and therefore we must reject
them. I will offer an alternative that does account for the biblical revelation.

The most prominent inadequate views of evangelists are

1. the church as the evangelist
2. the office of gospel writers
3. itinerant preachers of the Word
4. those with the spiritual gift of evangelism
5. ministers primarily to the lost, not the church
6. apostolic delegates
7. church planters/missionaries
8. the pastor does the work of the evangelist
9. evangelists cannot be distinguished from other officers
10. evangelists are "officers" with no defined office.

There are certainly other views, but these are the main ones. We will
examine each in light of the biblical testimony to expose their inadequacies
in describing Christ's gift to his church.

The Church as Evangelist

This first inadequate view is the topic of an entire book by George Sweazey by this title. The reason for addressing this error first is not because it is the most prominent but because it is representative of a shift in the terminology of the function of evangelists in our culture from the biblical usage. Our culture often uses the term *evangelist* when describing someone who speaks the gospel to others, but this is not in line with scriptural usage. Instead, those who speak the gospel to others are called ambassadors for Christ or simply regular Christians. The biblical term *evangelist* is reserved for a particular segment of the leadership who equip the body for living the Christian life.

Whatever may be worthy of commendation in Sweazey's thesis must be balanced with the reality that he made an unwarranted interpretive leap. In his own words, "Everything in this book rests on the conviction that *the Church is the Evangelist*."[269] Accordingly, everything in his book rests on a false conviction. This does not mean that there is nothing of value in his discussion, but the reality is that Jesus gave some to be evangelists according to Ephesians 4:11. This is explicitly contrary to Sweazey's conviction that the church—the whole body—was the evangelist. The church is called to evangelize the world; every member is supposed to participate and do his or her part as an ambassador. Even so, only some are evangelists. By mistakenly equating the different concepts of ambassadors and evangelists, Sweazey built his thesis on a faulty foundation.

Better terminology for Sweazey's view would be "the church as ambassador." All followers of Christ are called to be ambassadors for him. On the other hand, Jesus has given some as evangelists to equip the saints to walk in their individual stewardship of grace.

Sweazey affirmed, "The evangelist is not a person at all, but a fellowship."[270] Let us take this statement to the test of Scripture. In Acts 21:8, Philip was the evangelist. This is directly contrary to Sweazey's claim that the evangelist is not a person but a fellowship. Similarly, in 2 Timothy 4:5, Timothy was instructed to do the work of an evangelist. If Sweazey is correct, Timothy was being instructed to do the work of an

---

[269] Sweazey, *The Church As Evangelist*, xi, italics in original.
[270] Ibid., 47.

entire fellowship, not the work of an individual. This is contrary to the plain meaning of the text.

Whatever good may be gleaned from this hypothesis, the idea that the church is the evangelist must be rejected because it is expressly contrary to all three passages that explicitly describe the role and ministry of biblical evangelists.

Evangelists as the Office of Gospel Writers

A clear trend in the writings of some of the fathers of the church identified the authors of the canonical gospels as evangelists that some modern authors have picked up as well.[271] In an article dedicated to affirming this view, Dikran Hadidian set forth to "suggest a possible meaning to [the evangelists] as it is used in Eph 4:11, namely, that it stands for the 'office' of gospel writer and not just for the function of evangelization."[272] He concluded his study with an affirmation that this identification of evangelists as the office of gospel writers is indeed best.

Alastair Campbell remarked that Hadidian's article and thesis "has not received much support."[273] Regardless of the amount of support received, this view raises some valid historical observations regarding the use of the terminology of evangelists. After listing the three New Testament occurrences of the term, Hadidian cited Lindsay, who accurately observed that the terminology of evangelists is missing in the postapostolic literature, not being used in the Didache or in the apostolic fathers. The term *evangelist* does not turn up again until the writings of Tertullian and Eusebius, in the late second to early fourth centuries. This allows for a minimum of approximately one hundred years for the terminology to change. As a result, these writings cannot be the best source for our understanding *evangelist* as originally used by the biblical authors.

The historical usage of the term *evangelist* has certainly grown to include the writers of the canonical gospels. If we miss this point, we

---

[271] For example, DeSilva uses the term evangelist in this way; see DeSilva, *Introduction to the New Testament*.

[272] Hadidian, *"tous de euangelistas* in Eph 4,11," 317. This article presents a false dilemma, attempting to have us choose between two options that are false.

[273] Campbell, "Do the Work of an Evangelist," 117n2.

will likely misunderstand many authors throughout the history of the church and up to the present who refer to Matthew, Mark, Luke, and John as the evangelists. However, the biblical usage of the term makes this identification of the evangelists as those who fill the office of gospel writers impossible.

First, Philip was called "the evangelist" in Acts 21:8, but Philip did not write any of our canonical gospels. Second, Paul instructed Timothy to "do the work of an evangelist" in 2 Timothy 4:5. Timothy likewise did not write any of our canonical gospels, nor does the context of Paul's encouragement lend any credibility to the idea that he wanted him to.

While the terminology of evangelists undeniably changed over time to (at least) include the gospel writers, we must reject the view that the biblical term of evangelists was originally written to mean any such thing. The scope of the present chapter is not to define the historical evolution of the meaning of the term *evangelists* but to examine the biblical meaning. Accordingly, this view must likewise be rejected as inadequate for determining the biblical role and ministry of evangelists.

Evangelists as Itinerant Preachers

Another common view is that the evangelists were itinerant preachers. The number of commentators holding this view is large.[274] However, some commentators have been compelled to go against the grain of popular interpretation through examining the biblical data. Perhaps the best refutation of the present view is found in Earnest Best's work on Ephesians; he concluded, "The use of the word 'evangelist' in the N.T. provides then no direct evidence that it denotes travelling missionaries."[275]

By examining the life and ministry of Philip and Timothy, Best argued persuasively that the idea of the work of evangelists being tied to traveling

---

[274] See, for example, Mitton, *The New Century Bible Commentary*, 149–51; *The Interpreter's Bible Commentary*, 10:690–91; Erickson, *Evangelical Commentary on the Bible*, 1027; Gaebelein, *The Expositor's Bible Commentary*, 11:58; Thompson, *The Cambridge Bible Commentary on the NEB*, 68.

[275] Best, "Ministry in Ephesians," 153. Best also argued against the second inadequate view discussed above, namely that evangelists were intended in the Scriptures to refer to the office of gospel writers.

was false. Citing Best's analysis, Snodgrass stated that the notion of viewing the original evangelists as itinerants was probably not correct.[276] To claim that evangelists were traveling preachers, the biblical evidence must come from Philip's early ministry as he fled persecution in Jerusalem and moved toward Caesarea in Acts 8:4ff and then on the basis of his being called "the evangelist" in Acts 21:8. Yet we must wrestle with the reality that Philip was never called an evangelist during the description of his traveling evangelism. Instead, "at the time when he is termed evangelist in 21.8 he has an established home and his family are living with him in it; he is then no longer a travelling missionary."[277] We must account for the fact that if evangelists were itinerants, then the title *evangelist* was applied to Philip in a most perplexing place. We would be forced to conclude that Philip was described as a traveling missionary even though he no longer traveled as a missionary and had not done so for two decades.

The argument that Philip's identification as an evangelist harkens back to the activity described in Acts 8:4–40 is weak. Philip's ministry in Acts 8:4–40 was prefaced by these introductory remarks.

> Saul was in hearty agreement with putting him [Stephen] to death. And on that day a great persecution began against the church in Jerusalem, and they were all scattered throughout the regions of Judea and Samaria, except the apostles. Some devout men buried Stephen, and made loud lamentation over him. But Saul began ravaging the church, entering house after house, and dragging off men and women, he would put them in prison. Therefore, those who had been scattered went about preaching the word. (Acts 8:1–4)

The persecution caused all the believers—except the apostles—to be scattered, and those who were scattered went about preaching the Word. Philip comes into focus as an example of what was taking place, but the text does not indicate he was a preeminent example or some specially gifted

---

[276] Snodgrass, *The NIV Application Commentary.*

[277] Best, "Ministry in Ephesians," 152. See also Best's commentary on Ephesians.

person. The text does indicate Philip performed miraculous signs, but so did Stephen, who was also one of the seven.[278]

The most notable thing about Philip's preaching ministry was his entering Samaria and preaching to the Ethiopian eunuch, since the text tells us, "Those who were scattered because of the persecution that occurred in connection with Stephen made their way to Phoenicia and Cyprus and Antioch, speaking the word to no one except to Jews alone" (Acts 11:19). Philip was more like the smaller group described in the next verse: "But there were some of them, men of Cyprus and Cyrene, who came to Antioch and began speaking to the Greeks also, preaching the Lord Jesus" (Acts 11:20).

Though Philip was willing to preach to Samaritans and Gentiles sooner than some of his brothers and sisters in Christ, he was still simply doing what every other Christian (except the apostles) was doing at the same time: fleeing the persecution in Jerusalem and preaching the Word as he or she scattered throughout Judea and Samaria. Luke did not describe Philip as "one of the evangelists" in Acts 21:8 because such an idea was meaningless in the context. Philip's "ministry" described in Acts 8:4–40 would be better described as simply living a Christian lifestyle as an ambassador for Christ since it described all the Christians who were converted and trained under the apostles in Jerusalem between Pentecost and the martyrdom of Stephen. The training the Christians received from the apostles described in Acts 2:42 had each of them equipped and ready to boldly preach the Word when persecution struck. Philip eventually got to Caesarea in Acts 8:40; we have no indication that he ever traveled again. The next time we read about him in Acts 21:8, twenty years had passed and he was still in Caesarea.

If the interpretation that evangelists were traveling preachers is valid, the term *evangelist* could rightly be applied to every Christian who was not an apostle. They all traveled and proclaimed the Word as they went. This would make the usage of the term redundant and meaningless. We already know Philip was not one of the apostles. In addition, Ephesians 4:11 indicates that not all Christians were evangelists—only some were given as evangelists by Christ. All Christians are called to be ambassadors and walk in the ministry of reconciliation, which requires the proclamation

---

[278] Cf. Acts 8:5–13, 6:8.

of the gospel.[279] However, only some are called to equip the saints for this ministry as ambassadors. The apostles, prophets, evangelists, and pastors and teachers are the equippers of the saints for their work.[280]

Acts 21:8 also indicates that Philip was part of an exclusive group—one of the seven from Acts 6:1–6. This identification reminds us that his leadership qualities and spiritual qualifications were endorsed by the apostles and the body of believers when he was living in Jerusalem. It is a reasonable inference that Philip would become a recognized leader where he settled after the persecution, which was in Caesarea. As the early church continued to boldly share the gospel, Philip was not *an* evangelist among the rest who were silent; during the persecution, he was an ambassador among ambassadors since every Christian was preaching the Word wherever they went in obedience to the command of the risen Lord. After relocating, Philip became *the* evangelist in Caesarea. This is better understood as filling an important leadership role on a nonitinerant basis in a particular church setting, equipping, leading, and overseeing the saints in Caesarea to walk in the ministry of reconciliation they were called to by the risen Lord Jesus.

As we consider Timothy's call, we likewise see that the idea of a traveling preacher is far from what is described in the text. Best wrote, "When we look at 1 and 2 Timothy to see what roles Timothy was to fulfill we find he is expected to remain at Ephesus (1 Tim. 1.3), i.e. not to travel."[281]

The list of commentators who hold to the itinerant view of evangelists may be impressive, and many modern definitions of evangelists today call to mind those with an itinerant gospel ministry, but the evaluation of the biblical data does not support such a view. While it may be permissible and beneficial for some to travel and preach the gospel—and indeed some have fruitfully engaged in such ministry—it is inaccurate to affirm that the biblical function of evangelists is that of itinerant preachers of the gospel. Biblically speaking, Christ gave evangelists as a gift to his church, and they are better understood to be leaders in the local fellowship to fulfill their ministry to the body. Paul's expectation of Timothy's ministry duties "is

---

[279] 2 Cor 5:17–21.

[280] Eph 2:10, 4:1, 11–16.

[281] Best, "Ministry in Ephesians," 152–53.

accordingly related entirely to those who are already within the church (2 Tim. 4.2 offers a good summary) and it is within the church that he does the work of an evangelist."[282]

A subcategory of this view includes those with itinerant ministries to churches, not necessarily the lost. While this may be a valid form of ministry, traveling teachers who encourage and teach seminars do not fit the description of biblical evangelists by the same critique of the biblical function of evangelists as recognized, established, and continuing members of the local leadership team in an established church. Traveling teachers may be a beneficial ministry, but they are not the evangelists described in the Scriptures. Philip was dedicated to serving Caesarea, and Timothy's call to do the work of an evangelist was confined to Ephesus. No biblical example exists of an evangelist or one performing the work of an evangelist traveling beyond the limits of the local church to which he was called, so expanding the duties to include traveling would be speculative at best.

Upon examination, the view that evangelists are itinerant ministers, though popular, must be rejected as inadequate in light of the biblical testimony.

Evangelists as Those Gifted with the Spiritual Gift of Evangelism

This particular inadequate view has already been at least partially addressed, so I will consider it here only briefly.[283] This view is founded on the assertions of commentators who view the persons listed in Ephesians 4:11 as those gifted with the corresponding spiritual gifts. However, this assertion cannot be substantiated with the Scriptures because—particularly in the case of evangelists and evangelism—there is no biblical evidence that such a thing as a spiritual gift of evangelism exists. Evangelists exist, but this does not necessarily mean that evangelism must also exist as a spiritual gift. The burden of proof remains upon those who assert that evangelism is a spiritual gift, but no evidence exists beyond their assertions. Ephesians 4:11 does not list a spiritual gift of evangelism.

Certainly, an alternative explanation is possible as to the primary

---

[282] Ibid., 153.

[283] See chapter 7 and also the discussion in Kohler, *Gate Crashers*, 122–47.

spiritual gifting(s) for many evangelists: teaching and leadership, both explicitly listed as spiritual gifts (1 Cor 12; Rom 12), and leaders in general have the responsibility of teaching the body. Not all apostles, prophets, and pastors are given identical spiritual gifts to each other in the same group. Peter and Paul were differently gifted individuals though they were both apostles.

However, as leaders, all evangelists would be expected to teach and equip the body in fulfillment of their role described in Ephesians 4:12–16. Some commentators have even claimed that evangelists and pastor/teachers are two divisions of the leadership class of teachers mentioned in 1 Corinthians 12:28.[284] Millard Erickson wrote, "much of the teaching (the work of the clergy) was done by the apostles, prophets, and evangelists."[285] Erickson does not hold to the same view of evangelists as described in this book, but he indicated plainly that evangelists did a good amount of teaching in the early church.

To maintain that evangelists are those gifted with the spiritual gift of evangelism is to be dogmatic about an assertion that rests on the authority of commentators and with no explicit biblical text to build on. Instead, due to the overall teaching regarding leadership in the church combined with the purpose of all the other leadership roles in Ephesians 4:11 in fulfilling the purpose described in verses 12–16, it is better to view the biblical evangelist as a leader and a teacher and not as an individual who has the spiritual gift of evangelism.

Evangelists as Ministers to the Lost

This particular error is often held by those who mistakenly define the scope of the evangelist's ministry by a word study instead of the defining verses found in Ephesians 4:12–16. D. A. Carson warns about the dangers of this practice: "And in any case, specification of the meaning of a word on the sole basis of etymology can never be more than an educated guess."[286] When we mistakenly conclude that evangelists are those gifted with the spiritual gift of evangelism, this inadequate view is almost certainly the

---

[284] For example, *The Bible Commentary According to the Authorized Version*, 564.

[285] Erickson, *Christian Theology*, 1087.

[286] Carson, *Exegetical Fallacies*, 33.

next theological stop: evangelists, as Christians gifted in evangelism, should spend their time preaching to the lost and adding members to the church.

This seems reasonable at first glance; based on the culture we have received, it is considered self-evident. However, as demonstrated in the previous inadequate view, the ministry of evangelists as described in the Scriptures was primarily directed toward believers—the church—not toward unbelievers. This is exactly what Ephesians 4:12 says is the reason for Christ giving the gifts listed in 4:11—for the equipping of the saints, not for the conversion of the sinners.

Paul expressed that every Christian is supposed to serve in the ministry of reconciliation as an ambassador for Christ.[287] This is contrary to the views that attempt to restrict the ambassadorial function and ministry of reconciliation to only certain members of the body of Christ.[288] Therefore, the idea that only certain members of the body are gifted with evangelism and have a ministry to the lost is problematic and divisive.

In the same regard, when Paul encouraged Timothy to fulfill his ministry in Ephesus, "he is never instructed to seek the conversion of unbelievers."[289] As a minister to the church, Timothy's task was to get the church operating properly. When the body is equipped and built up, the whole body can perform their God ordained functions of proclaiming the gospel to the ends of the earth. This was not Timothy's job alone, nor the apostles, nor Philip's—it is the responsibility of the church as a whole. We all must be equipped to walk in the good works that God has prepared in advance for us to do.[290]

In this regard, the evangelist's function as described in the Bible is explicitly defined as a ministry to the saints, not to unbelievers. While this may seem counterintuitive and countercultural, it is very much in line with Jesus's prayer for the evangelization of the world and the spread of the knowledge of God to the ends of the earth.

Jesus prayed something truly astonishing in John 17:9: "I ask on their behalf; I do not ask on behalf of the world, but of those whom You have

---

[287] 2 Cor 5:17–21.

[288] For a more detailed discussion on the call for all Christians to live as ambassadors for Christ, see Kohler, *Gate Crashers*, 41–55.

[289] Best, "Ministry in Ephesians," 153.

[290] Cf. Eph 2:10 and 4:12–16.

given Me; for they are Yours." Jesus stated explicitly that he was not praying for the world but only for his disciples. While this may seem strange, Jesus later revealed the wide-ranging implication of this for the world in John 17:15–21.

> I do not ask You to take them out of the world, but to keep them from the evil one. They are not of the world, even as I am not of the world. Sanctify them in the truth; Your word is truth. As You sent Me into the world, I also have sent them into the world. For their sakes I sanctify Myself, that they themselves also may be sanctified in truth. I do not ask on behalf of these alone, but for those also who believe in Me through their word; that they may all be one; even as You, Father, are in Me and I in You, that they also may be in Us, so that the world may believe that You sent Me.

Note well that Jesus prayed for protection, sanctification, edification in the Word of God, and for their obedience in going into the world as Jesus himself was sent—to seek and save the lost, to testify to the truth, to testify that the world's deeds are evil, and to proclaim the kingdom of God and repentance and faith in the Messiah for the forgiveness of sins.[291] Jesus prayed not just for his original disciples but also for all who would believe through their word—which was Jesus praying directly for the church. Specifically, Jesus prayed for the unity of his current and future believers so that the world might believe through their testimony. It may seem like a long way around, but we must seriously and soberly wrap our minds around the reality that the church is God's intended vehicle for making his glory and gospel known to the ends of the earth.

Jesus did not pray some wishy-washy prayer for the salvation of the world. Instead, Jesus prayed for his church—that we would be unified, edified, and obedient to the commission—so that the world would come to know Jesus Christ was Lord and hear his command to all people to repent and trust in him alone for their salvation from God's wrath.

Would you be surprised to see that the risen Jesus gifted his church

---

[291] E.g., Luke 4:43, 19:10, 24:45–49; John 7:7; 18:37; etc.

with apostles, prophets, evangelists, and pastor/teachers for the same purpose of building unity, maturity, knowledge of the Son, and love among the body so the church would be equipped to share the gospel with all creation? To reduce the ministry of evangelists to the lost is to critically damage Jesus's design for edifying and building up the body. It often results in the catastrophic theological perspective that evangelism is best left to the professionals. That is foolish.

When we think evangelists minister primarily to the lost, we do a disservice to the biblical testimony that all Christians are to live as ambassadors and ministers of reconciliation to a lost world in the name of Jesus. I am as guilty as anyone else in using the term *evangelist* for those who preach the gospel to nonbelievers just as I use the word *church* to describe a building. The body would be edified by changing our terminology to describe those who are preaching to the lost as ambassadors instead of as evangelists because evangelists' primary ministry according to the Scriptures is to the church, not the lost. Evangelists, like every other member of the body, are also ambassadors for Christ, but not all ambassadors are evangelists. The whole world will hear faster and more efficiently if every Christian is equipped to boldly and lovingly share the gospel than if the work of evangelization is left only to some.

Evangelists as Apostolic Delegates

This view is also fairly common among the commentators and was the most prominent view during the Reformation.[292] Apostolic delegates would have died out after the apostolic age since they carried on their work in subordination to the apostles and under the coordination of the apostles. Since the apostles did not continue, so also the evangelists did not continue into the subsequent generations. In this view, Timothy is the perfect example of an evangelist because he was Paul's apostolic delegate to Ephesus and was tasked with responsibilities greater than any pastor, elder, or overseer would receive. In this view, the evangelist was temporary and extraordinary (as were the prophets and apostles) higher than the pastor/

---

[292] Lange notes that despite being prevalent among the reformers, this view is untenable in *Lange's Commentary on the Holy Scriptures* (NT), 7:149–50.

teacher, and not for today. Many prominent leaders throughout church history have held this view.[293]

Often commentators who take this (or a related) view then garner further evidence for their position by asserting that others such as Epaphras[294] were evangelists. Yet we should be very careful when we define our terms and then assign our titles to others we think fit our description when the Bible never does.

Only one person was actually, indisputably, called an evangelist in the Bible (Philip, Acts 21:8). Only one person was told to do the work of an evangelist (Timothy; 2 Tim 4:5). The risen and exalted Lord Jesus gave some to be evangelists (Eph 4:11). Based on the biblical data, it is difficult to maintain that evangelists are apostolic delegates because this identification does not fit the one person we know for sure to be an evangelist, Philip.

The fact that there were apostolic delegates—Timothy, Titus, Crescens, and the like—is not in dispute. In fact, to describe Timothy as an apostolic delegate instead of pastor might be the best and most accurate terminology. Yet if Timothy had been an apostolic delegate, Paul's admonition for him to "do the work of an evangelist" is a meager foundation for asserting that evangelists are the same as apostolic delegates. As apostolic delegates, their ministry responsibilities would be defined by the apostle who sent them for a particular purpose. Different situations may call for different assignments. Indeed, we have no record of Paul telling Titus or any of his other delegates to "do the work of an evangelist."

What we do have record of is an apostle instructing one of his delegates to do the work of an evangelist; it is thus an unjustified leap to say all apostolic delegates were evangelists. Timothy was instructed to do the work of an evangelist while he remained in Ephesus. If Timothy was an evangelist, he would not only have to have done the work of an evangelist in Ephesus but also would have been an evangelist at all times by nature of his ministry as an apostolic delegate. If this is true, the exhortation from Paul becomes unnecessary. More important, Philip was clearly defined as an evangelist (not merely told to do the work of one), yet we never see him

---

[293] E.g., John Calvin and John Wesley. See Carter, *The Wesleyan Bible Commentary*, 5:410; Calvin, *Calvin's Commentaries*, 21:279–80.

[294] E.g., Gaebelein, *The Expositor's Bible Commentary*, 11:58.

being specifically under the charge of an apostle in the same sense that Timothy, Titus, and Silas were.

In light of the biblical evidence, it is difficult to maintain that evangelists were apostolic delegates because the only indisputable evangelist, Philip, was not an apostolic delegate. In fact, the apostles followed Philip to Samaria; he was not sent by them. He traveled there as a result of the persecution under Saul, and he was preaching and performing miracles, something Timothy was never recorded as doing in the inspired text. Peter and John were sent to verify and put an apostolic stamp of approval on this movement away from preaching to Jews only, but to say Philip was an apostolic delegate to Samaria or Caesarea would be an unjustifiable leap.

Therefore, the view that evangelists were extraordinary and noncontinuing likewise falls away. Philip's role as an evangelist was not directly tied to any direct apostolic delegation or sending. As a result, we have no reason to believe evangelists passed away after the apostolic age and have not continued to the present. As such, this view must be rejected.

Evangelists as Church Planters and Missionaries

This view is similar to the previous one, but it allows for the continuation of the evangelists to the present. In this view, evangelists are what we would think of as church planters and missionaries—those who take the gospel to new territory and further the advance of the kingdom of God. Some variations of this perspective consider evangelists as a sort of continuation of the apostolic ministry but without the foundational or revelatory function. There is also great overlap with this definition and what some refer to as modern-day apostles or apostolic workers.[295]

Historically, the term *evangelist* takes on this meaning at a fairly early date. Writing in the third to fourth century, Eusebius stated,

> Then starting out upon long journeys they performed the office of evangelists, being filled with the desire to preach Christ to those who had not yet heard the word of faith, and to deliver to them the divine Gospels. And when they had only laid the foundations of the faith in foreign

---

[295] E.g., Viola, *Finding Organic Church*, chapter 2.

places, they appointed others as pastors, and entrusted them with the nurture of those that had recently been brought in, while they themselves went on again to other countries and nations, with the grace and the co-operation of God.[296]

For some, this evidence is overwhelmingly conclusive. Eusebius is an early source who clearly equated the missionary work of traveling to where the gospel had not been preached, planting churches, and establishing leadership in the form of pastors before moving on to do it again as a description of "performing the office of evangelists."[297] I have no doubt this is what the office of evangelist became. Yet the purpose of this study is not a sketch of the historical development of the office of evangelist as intriguing as that may be. Instead, we are attempting to discern the nature of Christ's gift to his church as originally defined in the Scriptures.

This view is similar to the itinerant view above, but these views are not identical. An itinerant minister travels almost exclusively, settling only for short periods. The itinerant model often views the responsibility of evangelists only as preachers with no administrative or governing oversight.[298] The current view being examined gives more governing authority to evangelists, placing them above the pastor/teacher because evangelists have the authority to appoint the pastor/teacher before moving on and settling in the next area for as long as necessary to establish another self-governing church body.

However, this view falters because Timothy was sent to an established church community in Ephesus. If the work of an evangelist originally included going where the gospel had not been preached to establish a church, Timothy was being charged with an impossible task; the gospel had come to Ephesus and the church was alive and well. Whatever Paul meant in his charge to Timothy to do the work of an evangelist, he could not have meant what Eusebius understood the subsequent generations of "evangelists" to be.

Those who emphasize the authority of historical interpretation may find

---

[296] Eusebius, *Church History*, III, 37:2–3.

[297] *TDNT* follows in this understanding of evangelists.

[298] E.g., *The Bible Commentary According to the Authorized Version*, 564.

it difficult to move past Eusebius's clear definition despite its conflict with biblical data. Two statements must be made here: first, words often change meaning rapidly. Do you remember the television show *The Flintstones*? I guarantee that if that show were airing today, they would change the lyrics to their theme song lest people get the wrong idea about the topic matter of the show. This radical shift in the primary meaning of the word *gay* has occurred in less than fifty years. Eusebius was writing more than two hundred years after Paul—is it really that hard to imagine that the word *evangelist* could have taken on different nuance during that time?

Second, consider the fact that the local churches the apostle Paul himself founded began to go astray during his life. Paul had to severely reprimand the Galatian churches as well as the saints in Corinth for their foolish straying from biblical ideals and apostolic teaching. If this happened during the lifetime of the apostles, we should have no problem accepting that Eusebius's definition—while helpful for describing contemporaneous usage of the terminology and interesting as a look at the historical development of the office of evangelist—could likewise have deviated from apostolic usage. As a result, historical examples should by no means cause us to redefine the office of evangelist as originally designed by Christ and given for his church if we can find clear definition in the Bible.

Indeed, we see that with other offices and terms in Scripture (where we have more-robust biblical data) the meaning has changed a great deal in less time than passed between the writing of the New Testament and Eusebius. Commentators are nearly unanimous that the biblical usage of bishop/overseer[299] and elder[300] refer to the same office or leadership function.[301] Yet despite the strong biblical case for the equivalence of these terms, we see that in less than thirty years after the death of the last apostle, there was an emerging divide between these terms with the elevation of the office of the bishop over and above the elders in the writings of Ignatius.[302]

---

[299] Gk: ἐπίσκοπος (*episkopos*).

[300] Gk: πρεσβύτερος (*presbyteros*).

[301] See, e.g., Merkle, *40 Questions About Elders and Deacons*, 54–58; Grudem, *Systematic Theology*, 912–16; Geisler, *Systematic Theology*, 4:111–13; Knight, "Two Offices," 1–12; etc.

[302] For a good overview of this historical shift, see Geisler, *Systematic Theology*, 4:127–32. See also, Viola and Barna, *Pagan Christianity?* chapter 5.

We must recognize both the value and the limits of history and tradition. When tradition preserves and embodies biblical truth as delivered by the apostles, we should cling to it. When tradition and history deviate from the apostolic tradition, we should reject it and not allow it to nullify the Word of God. In this case, the biblical data makes the view of evangelists as church planters and missionaries impossible. Therefore, this view must be discarded as inadequate in relationship to the biblical role of evangelists.

The Pastor Does the Work of the Evangelist

Some who interpret Timothy to be the pastor of the church at Ephesus consequently see Paul's statement as a commandment to pastors to do the work of evangelists. Often in my discussions with church leaders, this objection is raised explicitly by pastors who say, "It's my job to equip the church to evangelize, to lead the charge, and to preach the Word faithfully and boldly. As the pastor, I am called to do the work of an evangelist." Included in this interpretation is the evidence of its own falsity: pastors and leaders who hold this interpretation must affirm that the work of an evangelist is different from the work of a pastor to conclude that they are the same, which is to commit the fallacy of equivocation.

If equipping the saints and leading the charge in evangelism is the work of the pastor, why did Paul encourage Timothy to do the work of an evangelist and not the work of a pastor? For Paul, the work of an evangelist was distinct from the work of a pastor. Likewise, if pastors and evangelists were the same, Paul would not have written that Jesus gave some apostles, some prophets, some evangelists, and some pastors and teachers.[303] This view must be rejected as inadequate, and it naturally leads into the next view.

Evangelists Cannot be Distinguished from other Officers

Though the distinction may be ill-defined or hidden to us, it was not so to Paul or Timothy. Based on his instruction to Timothy and his letter to the saints in Ephesus, Paul had a well-defined difference in role in his

---

[303] Eph 4:11.

mind between the functions in Ephesians 4:11, which worked together toward edifying the body and uniting the saints.

Simply because something is not obvious to us at first does not mean that the best conclusion is to say there is nothing to distinguish these different things. To honor the Scriptures as written and inspired, we must recognize we have received two terms in the same context: Christ gave some evangelists and some pastor/teachers. These are different groups of leaders, and we can affirm they are different even if we might not be able to fully define their differences. Therefore, to conclude they cannot be differentiated is faulty. These officers can in fact be differentiated simply by the designations we have received in Ephesians 4:11, which indicate Paul intended for them to be differentiated.

Evangelists as Officers with No Defined "Office"

If we acknowledge that there is at least some difference between pastors and evangelists (as the different terms suggest), a secondary difficulty is raised by some commentators in defining their particular roles. Earnest Best affirmed that the roles of evangelist, shepherd, and teacher were not clearly distinguishable.[304] Often, those who affirm that the evangelists have no official office described[305] do not recognize one (evangelists) but uphold the other (pastors) in local church leadership roles—which is selective interpretation at its clearest. However, it is irresponsible to eliminate a leader that Christ gave simply because a definition of their role may temporarily elude us.

Part of the difficulty is that the purpose(s) of the leaders listed in Ephesians 4:11 are all tied to the same purpose in 4:12–16. Paul did not expound on the differences between the work of an apostle, the work of a prophet, the work of an evangelist, and the work of a pastor/teacher; he simply told us Christ had given these officers as a gift to his church.

Clearly defining their ministry duties was never his purpose. Paul's purpose in Ephesians 4:11 was to provide inspired revelation regarding Jesus's design for his church—these are the gifts Jesus gave for leading his

---

[304] Best, *International Critical Commentary*, 389.
[305] E.g., Nelson, *The Century Bible Commentary*, 19.

church, and those who fill these roles should be known and established as leaders so they can equip the body.

Those called to these roles may have different responsibilities.[306] For example, Jesus called Peter and Paul to be apostles, but their responsibilities and the scope of their ministries were different. The same is true for the apostles Peter and John. When Jesus told Peter part of his responsibilities in John 21, Jesus rebuked Peter for being so concerned about what John's particular calling was.[307] The apostles served whatever leadership role was necessary in their spheres of influence just as pastors have the same general call of leadership and oversight while not always doing it in the same way as other pastors, and teachers have the responsibility to edify the body but are not required to follow the same curriculum.

When Jesus gives a gift to his church, we can trust he will lead them to fulfill their ministry. This is not to say that there is not a general outline of responsibilities that applies to apostles, prophets, evangelists, and pastor/teachers respectively, but we may easily get off track by seeking to overly define these leadership roles.

In general terms, we can see that the apostles and prophets had foundational roles[308] (at least) and that the continuing functions of the evangelists and pastor/teachers were based in the local church and built on the foundation of Christ, the apostles, and prophets. Since evangelists and pastor/teachers seek to edify the church, we should not be surprised to find that the purpose of the church to gather for instruction and edification and to scatter for the proclamation of the gospel would have leaders appointed to oversee each of the major tasks of the church in general.

The church must be instructed, edified, and led in the internal and external call of the church alike.[309] Praise God for his gifts of leaders for each major area of responsibility! How these particular leaders lead and govern will be a product of their particular gifting and ministry context. When we recognize the gifts, they will do what they are supposed to do. Of course, leaders who neglect or abuse their positions must be rebuked,

---

[306] Rom 14:4.

[307] John 21:18–23.

[308] Eph 2:20.

[309] See chapter 3.

corrected, or removed as is the topic of many other biblical passages and teaching on the relationship between leaders and the body in general.

If you are not an evangelist, it is likely difficult for you to understand what an evangelist might do. The same is true of pastors. Many regular church attenders have no idea what their pastors do daily. If you were to compare the schedules and activities of different church pastors, you would likely find many areas of overlap and divergence. As I look at the ministry of Paul, I often simply can't relate because I'm not an apostle. I am a pastor and teacher. As I co-lead a congregation in partnership with my other elders under the headship of Christ, my evangelist and I do not see everything the same way nor do we spend our time in the same pursuits. He's an evangelist, and I'm a pastor.

When we recognize the leadership of the right people Jesus has given for his church and allow them the freedom to be whom Christ has made them to be, amazing fruitfulness can result. As they demonstrate their faithfulness and call, the body is called to willfully submit to their leadership.[310] False apostles, prophets, evangelists, and pastors and teachers are real dangers and should be avoided at all costs and should be removed quickly when they emerge through church discipline with the hope they will repent and be restored to fellowship. The existence of these false counterparts only heightens the importance and need for the genuine ones to be properly recognized and established in churches for the edification of the body and the protection and dissemination of the gospel. This was God's design for doing abundantly more than all we can ask or think through his power that is at work in the church.[311]

Despite claims to the contrary, the office and role of evangelists are defined as distinct from the other members of Ephesians 4:11. While there is clearly going to be some overlap in leadership responsibilities,[312] this does not then nullify the differences. It is a logical and interpretive error to assert that because some of the responsibilities, tasks, and functions are the same (or similar) that therefore there is no distinction between them. Microwave ovens and jet airplanes both have glass, metal, buttons,

---

[310] E.g., Heb 13:17.

[311] Eph 3:20–21.

[312] E.g., teaching is shared by all the ministries in Eph 4:11.

displays, and require electricity, but the similarities do not mean that these two things cannot still be differentiated; the differences are significant.[313]

It could easily be argued that without adequate pastor/teachers in any fellowship, there will be a steady drift toward false doctrine with no one to soundly refute false teachers and to protect against every wind and wave of doctrine. Similarly, it has also been observed that "a church always tends to drift away from evangelism, never toward it."[314] This is not the case when there is an evangelist as part of the leadership team. It is impossible to drift from evangelism when there is an acknowledged and recognized evangelist on duty in a church. In these cases, those who want to drift from evangelism need to find an evangelist-free church.

After taking a closer look, all these views are likewise inadequate.

Conclusion

The major views on evangelists are all lacking. Should we therefore give up and simply stop talking about this? By no means! Despite the lack of a genuinely biblical description of evangelists being widely agreed upon, all the elements have already been discussed and are present in the discussion. The dots just have not been fully connected in a way that is faithful to the biblical revelation. In the next chapter, I will attempt to provide a description of the original design of evangelists by Jesus for his church as revealed in the Scriptures.

---

[313] I am not sure if I made this up or if I picked this illustration up from somewhere, but it helps illustrate the point.

[314] Booth, "Evangelism in the Home Church," 171.

CHAPTER 9

Evangelists and Christ's Church

He is also head of the body, the church; and He is the
beginning, the firstborn from the dead, so that He Himself
will come to have first place in everything.
—Colossians 1:18

It would be inappropriate to simply point out the inadequacies of the various views on the table without attempting to present a viable understanding of evangelists as given by Jesus for his church. An adequate view will take into account all the available biblical data and offer some explanatory ability for dealing with some of the extrabiblical phenomena. One important example is answering the following question: if evangelists were so important in the apostolic church, why is there no mention of them again until the third century?

Only three passages explicitly mention evangelists—Acts 21:8, Ephesians 4:11, and 2 Timothy 4:5—and we have already looked at each from various angles. We must remember, however, that the New Testament is not a how-to manual on church government or a systematic theology. It has been well said, "Whoever knows only the Book / Does not know the Book."[315] If we simply study the content of the Scriptures without understanding its context, we will often misunderstand the intended meaning of the text.[316] As we try to understand the intended purpose and

---

[315] This saying is hesitantly attributed to Frank Marshall in Parrott, "New Testament Elders in their Context," 27–28.

[316] A good place to start for anyone desiring to see how the New Testament documents fit together in one flowing historical narrative is encouraged to read Viola, *The*

role for evangelists in the church, we should keep in mind the basic flow of the apostle Paul's ministry and his relationship to those he was writing to.[317]

As Paul traveled as a preacher of the gospel, he was intentional about forming and strengthening communities of believers—churches—that would continue to live as light in the darkness and spread the good news of the gospel well after Paul was gone. Two of the places Paul spent the most time were Corinth and Ephesus. Paul wrote to the saints in Ephesus during his first Roman imprisonment, and his letter would have been received by the saints in Ephesus after not having seen Paul for five years.[318] Yet as many commentators have rightly observed, the tone of Ephesians seems oddly impersonal considering the amount of time Paul spent with them previously and the great emotion Paul and the elders from Ephesus expressed when they wept together thinking it was likely the last time they would see each other.[319]

Though several alternatives have been proposed for the lack of personal touch, it could simply be explained by the growth of the church. As Paul had been absent for half a decade, they had grown significantly. At the time of writing, their leadership and body was composed of many members who had never met Paul but had only heard of him.

An alternative interpretation that seems even more likely to me is that our canonical letter to the Ephesians was originally intended to be shared by all the churches in Asia Minor. This view explains the lack of personal touch more convincingly while also accounting for the absence of the words *in Ephesus* from several important early manuscripts of Ephesians 1:1. This view also strengthens the observations made about the importance of the role of evangelists in the local church leadership structure, since it would indicate that evangelists were recognized not just in Ephesus but also in all the churches the letter was intended to reach.

Untold Story of the New Testament.

[317] I must acknowledge the excellent book by Barentsen, *Emerging Leadership*. Though Barentsen and I do not reach all the same conclusions, I found his study on the leadership in Paul's churches illuminating.

[318] Not everyone agrees on this dating. For a good overview see Guthrie, *New Testament Introduction*, 489–95.

[319] Acts 20:17–38.

No matter the audience—just Ephesus or all the churches in Asia Minor—I agree with Barentsen that Paul's letter does not read as an instruction manual in how to arrange church leadership.[320] Instead, Paul described a leadership structure that was in place and recognized by the recipients—a structure that recognized the authority and role of apostles, prophets, evangelists, and pastor/teachers. Paul did not urge the recipients to adopt this system or to appoint these leaders because that was the leadership structure they already knew, practiced, and recognized.

This is contrary to Paul's approach in writing to the saints in Corinth, where Paul was dealing with a challenge to his apostolic authority. To the Corinthians, Paul affirmed that he was called an apostle by Jesus Christ in both his canonical letters to them, and he urged them to acknowledge his apostolic calling and not be led astray by false apostles. The ability for the Corinthians to benefit from the apostle was directly tied to their acknowledgment of his authority from Christ, bestowed upon Paul for their benefit. (The last sentence is worth rereading.)

Paul plainly stated in Ephesians 4:11 that Christ had given not just apostles but also prophets, evangelists, and pastor/teachers—and he assumed the saints were aware of these gifts from Christ for the equipping of the church. He did not urge them to accept these persons, acknowledge them, or submit to them. Unlike his letters to the Corinthians, Ephesians took for granted that the saints in Ephesus already understood this, so Paul disclosed the glorious purpose of Christ's leadership gifts and explained how important they were to the proper growth and functioning of the body and the fulfillment of God's glorious purpose in the church.

This view—that these roles and functions in Ephesians 4:11 were known and understood by Paul's contemporaries—is further strengthened by the reality that Paul could instruct Timothy to do the work of an evangelist and expect Timothy to understand him without further explanation. Timothy had a preexisting awareness of what an evangelist ought to do. Paul could also expect the saints in Ephesus to recognize and submit to Timothy's work as an evangelist just as they were submitting to his other duties as Paul's delegate.

In contrast to the disunity and problems experienced in Corinth, the health of the body in Ephesus can be linked to the proper identification

---

[320] Barentsen, *Emerging Leadership*.

and acknowledgment of and submission to Christ's appointed leadership.[321] This does not imply a blind submission to an office regardless of who fills it; quite the contrary. The Corinthian believers were foolishly being led astray by false apostles, illustrating the reality that submitting to usurpers of a biblical office was a major source of error. The remedy to this problem is a proper recognition of those persons Christ has actually given for performing the particular functions of leadership among the saints.

What is particularly interesting in his letter to the Ephesians is that Paul appealed to a leadership structure but never mentioned elders, overseers, or deacons. Prior to writing the letter to the Ephesians, when Paul called for the leadership of Ephesus to meet him at Miletus, he sent for the elders.[322] After writing Ephesians, in his letter to Timothy (who was serving in Ephesus), Paul discussed the importance of spiritually qualified elders and deacons.[323] When writing to the church in Philippi, Paul addressed the letter to all the saints, including the overseers and deacons.[324] When he left Titus on Crete, he told him to establish elders in every city.[325] This was consistent with Paul's practice of appointing elders in every church he planted.[326] Failing to mention elders, overseers, or deacons while discussing leadership has caused some commentators to question whether Paul wrote this letter to the Ephesians because the leadership structure seems to be contrary to what we find throughout the New Testament, not just in the writings of Paul.[327]

The consistent New Testament pattern of church government was a plurality of elders in every church.[328] Some (including Strong and Erickson[329]) contend that the church need not follow this pattern since

---

[321] For a similar teaching, see Heb 13:7, 17.

[322] Acts 20:17.

[323] 1 Tim 3:1–13.

[324] Phil 1:1.

[325] Titus 1:5.

[326] Acts 14:23.

[327] I will simply affirm that I hold to Pauline authorship and am not persuaded by any of the arguments that attempt to cast doubt on this. For an extended discussion see Guthrie, *New Testament Introduction*, chapter 13.

[328] See, e.g., Geisler, *Systematic Theology*, 4:104–45; Grudem, *Systematic Theology*, 904–49; Merkle, *40 Questions About Elders and Deacons*, 161–68.

[329] E.g., Erickson, *Christian Theology*, 1079–97.

they believe the model is merely descriptive, not prescriptive. In this particular matter, I believe them to be in error. Grudem has appropriately asked, "Why should we follow Strong and adopt as the norm a pattern of church government which is *nowhere* found in the New Testament, and reject a pattern *everywhere* found in the New Testament?"[330]

We should not. In attempting to argue for a singular elder model of local church government—the "senior pastor" model—examples are given of James in Jerusalem, Titus on Crete, and Timothy in Ephesus. Grudem refuted all these examples by pointing out that in Jerusalem, Crete, and Ephesus, "we know there were *elders* (plural) in the churches involved."[331] We know that, whatever James was,[332] there was undoubtedly a plurality of eldership along with the apostles in Jerusalem.[333] Similarly, whatever Timothy's exact role was in Ephesus, we know the church in Ephesus had elders (plural) and deacons in leadership.[334] Likewise, Titus was tasked with appointing elders in every town.[335] The case has been adequately made elsewhere, so I will merely affirm the reality for the sake of clarity: in the New Testament, we see a universal pattern of apostles establishing self-governing churches under a plurality of elders.

So why did the epistle to the Ephesians not discuss elders but only apostles, prophets, evangelists, and pastors and teachers? We must pay careful attention to the details in the text. A pattern emerged in Paul's ministry and in his instruction to his delegates regarding elders—they were to be appointed based on spiritual qualifications. Paul exhorted Timothy and Titus to appoint elders using specific criteria, and Paul himself appointed elders for every church he established in Lystra, Iconium, and Pisidian Antioch on his "first missionary journey."[336] However, when describing the leaders in Ephesians 4:11, Paul used different language. Instead of "appointing" these leaders, Paul stated they had been "given"

---

[330] Grudem, *Systematic Theology*, 930, italics in original.

[331] Ibid., 930–31, italics in original.

[332] Pastor, apostle, elder, or some combination of these; see, e.g., 1 Cor 15:7; Gal 1:19.

[333] Acts 15:2.

[334] Acts 20:17; 1 Tim 1:3, 3:1–13, 5:17–20.

[335] Titus 1:5.

[336] Acts 14:21–23.

by Jesus himself. Jesus gives apostles, prophets, evangelists, and pastor/ teachers, and he does so for the edification of his church.

In Corinth, there were questions regarding Paul's apostolic authority. Even so, Paul's authority as an apostle was not based on the recognition of it by the Corinthians. Paul's authority had been divinely appointed by the risen Jesus; it was not the result of a normal maturation process but was conferred on him at his conversion.[337] However, any benefit the Corinthians would receive from Paul would come from their rightly recognizing and submitting to his divinely appointed authority. This is why Paul urged them to recognize his apostolic authority and to reject the false apostles who were trying to lead them astray.

Paul wanted the Corinthians to properly recognize the authority and gift that Jesus had given them, and the gift was Paul himself as their apostle. What we see in Paul's expressed theology to the saints at Ephesus is not different from the patterns we have seen before; it was an expression of the same truth from a different angle.

According to Paul, Jesus had given some as apostles, some as prophets, some as evangelists, and some as pastors and teachers for the leadership of his church, for the equipping of the saints, and for the edification of the whole body. Based on this foundational understanding, Paul instructed churches to recognize these leaders through official appointments for the benefit of the church. When false apostles, false prophets, or false teachers gain positions of influence, the results can be catastrophic. As a result, Paul was confident that when God saved individuals through his grace and established fellowships of believers, he did not leave them as orphans but would bestow special gifts of grace in the form of the leadership roles in Ephesians 4:11. It then became the serious and sober responsibility of the body to recognize and publicly appoint these leaders and to submit to

---

[337] See Jesus' description of Paul's ministry calling as told to Ananias in Acts 9:15–16 immediately following his conversion. The point is that the calling was from Jesus; since he is sovereign, we must not be dogmatic in thinking everyone called to be an apostle, prophet, evangelist, or pastor/teacher likewise had to walk in this calling from the moment of conversion. The Lord may have reasons to delay some individuals calling into the Ephesians 4:11 ministries, like the course that happened with Philip from convert to deacon to evangelist over many years. Even with Paul, it took more than a decade before he began walking fully in his calling as an apostle of Jesus.

them but also to hold them accountable if the church wished to flourish under God's design. Over time, as these leaders are functioning properly, it should result in the body growing together in maturity, leading to more individuals growing to positions of oversight and teaching from within the fellowship.

As the function of apostles and prophets was foundational, these roles have not continued to the present day in person; the apostolic and prophetic foundation has been preserved for us in the Scriptures. Geisler affirmed this reality several times in his *Systematic Theology*, and many other commentators went to great lengths to reserve the apostles and prophets in Ephesians 2:20 and 3:5 to New Testament prophets—therefore, this foundation is specifically found in the New Testament. Of course, the apostles and prophets[338] were already operating on the assumption that the Old Testament was God's Word, so they did not worry about making a case for the foundational and enduring nature of these writings, which were simply assumed.[339]

In this respect—through both the Old and New Testament—the continuing role of apostles and prophets are included in all churches as the foundation, with Jesus himself as the cornerstone.[340] Without Christ, you don't have a church. If you attempt to take the Scriptures out of a church, the negative consequences for unity, maturity, knowledge of the Son of God, and love will be many.

According to Paul, Christ's design for local church leadership, edification, and mobilization also included evangelists and pastor/teachers to build on the apostolic and prophetic foundation. If Paul's theology led him to believe Christ gave both evangelists and pastor/teachers for the proper equipping and functioning of each church, it follows that he would look for them and publicly appoint them for the benefit of the church.

This reconstruction of Paul's theology explains why every church, then, should have a plurality of elders: every church should have a pastor/teacher and an evangelist (at least) in addition to being built on the foundation of the apostles and prophets in the faith handed down to

---

[338] E.g., Luke and Mark, who were not apostles.
[339] E.g., 2 Tim 3:14–17; 2 Pet 3:1–3.
[340] Eph 2:20.

the saints.[341] Speaking pragmatically, a small church does not necessarily need a plurality of pastors; a small group of believers can adequately be shepherded and overseen by one. Yet, if Jesus intended for two types of overseers—an evangelist overseer and a pastor/teacher overseer—even the smallest church would require a plurality of elders/overseers because both functions need to be filled for the body of Christ to be properly equipped and shepherded into the fullness of Christ.

As Knight capably demonstrated, every officer listed in Ephesians 4:11 was an elder.[342] The apostles John and Peter began referring to themselves as elders later in their ministry.[343] Similarly, a common qualification of elders was their need to be hospitable.[344] When Paul and his ministry companions arrived in Caesarea, they stayed in the house of Philip the evangelist—a man who was previously recognized when he served in Jerusalem as someone of good reputation and full of the Spirit and of wisdom, thus demonstrating a character in line with the requirements given to Timothy and Titus by Paul.[345] Contrary to the modern notions of evangelists as itinerant preachers and therefore those needing hospitality on their travels, we see the evangelist in the Scriptures extended hospitality and opened his home to traveling workers.

This understanding also answers the question of why the term *evangelist* seemingly disappeared historically in the period immediately following the time of the apostles. The answer is simply because the term *elders* included both pastors and evangelists under its scope. Apostles, prophets, evangelists, and pastor/teachers were different functions that all operated in the singular office of elder/overseer.

While all apostles are elders, not all elders are apostles. In the same way, while all evangelists are elders, not all elders are evangelists. Therefore, it becomes natural in calling for or describing the leadership of the church in general to refer to the elders—a term that includes apostles, prophets, evangelists, pastors and teachers, and any other elders who exercise oversight or provide leadership. When beneficial or necessary to maintain

---

[341] Jude 1:3.

[342] Knight, "Two Offices."

[343] E.g., 1 Pet 5:1; 2 John 1:1; 3 John 1:1.

[344] 1 Tim 3:2; Titus 1:8.

[345] Acts 6:3–5.

the separate titles that point to a particular function, this was done in the text. Philip was an elder; in particular, he was an evangelist. It is not unnatural to refer to him as the evangelist (which entails he was an elder) so the church would understand his function and submit to his leadership in that particular regard for their blessing and edification.

Each separate title takes on a particular nuance in referring to each particular area of oversight. Since apostles and prophets are foundational, their eldership and oversight extends to every church.[346] In contrast, the remaining elders are tied to the local church they serve. In a particular church, the area of oversight for evangelists would be tied to the external mission of the church, namely, equipping and leading the body of Christ in proclaiming the gospel to everyone. Conversely, the area of oversight for the pastor/teacher would be tied to the internal mission of the church— shepherding the saints and the instruction and equipping of the body in regard to doctrine and faith, including correcting false doctrine.

When Paul wrote to the saints in Ephesus, whom we know had elders, he stated plainly that Jesus gave some as apostles, some as prophets, some as evangelists, and some as pastors and teachers; they knew he was referring to their elders. When Paul wanted to meet with the leadership, he simply called for the elders to meet him.[347] Based on this reconstruction, there was no hint of disagreeing forms of leadership described or discussed.

The proposed understanding of Paul's theology of leadership explains some gaps in our understanding. It also gives us further insight into the role and function of evangelists, especially if they are now to be considered as part of the elders and leaders as discussed in other biblical passages. While some may object to this inclusion, usually, no objection is raised to the pastor being included in the elder/overseer discussion. The burden of proof rests on those who would include pastors but disqualify evangelists from passages such as Hebrews 13:17 or 1 Peter 5:1–3 to explain their justification biblically.

Though you'd never know it by looking at our modern church leadership structures, scripturally speaking, we have three times as much

---

[346] Peter (the apostle to the Jews) had no problem writing to churches planted by the apostle Paul (the apostle to the Gentiles), urging them to remember the words of their apostles (plural); 1 Pet 1:1; 2 Pet 3:1–2.

[347] E.g., Acts 20:17.

textual evidence for the importance and role of evangelists in leadership than we do for pastors, as they are mentioned in Acts 21:8, 2 Timothy 4:5, and Ephesians 4:11. We have no biblical evidence beyond Ephesians 4:11 that anyone was ever actually called a "pastor"—other than Jesus, that is.[348] Though some assert that Timothy, Titus, and James were pastors, we must acknowledge there is no text explicitly calling them pastors. In contrast, we know that at least Caesarea had a recognized evangelist (Philip), and Timothy was doing the work of an evangelist in Ephesus.

The office of elder is broader than simply including the gifts given by Jesus in Ephesians 4:11, but it is not less than this. If we desire to move toward a pure governmental form in our local churches, we should recognize and appoint those with the leadership gifts Jesus has given. We should also affirm and recognize that growth and spiritual maturity are expected from every Christian, not just the leadership. Therefore, Paul affirmed and expected that a plurality of elders would be present in each congregation because Jesus gave these gifts for the building up of his body in accordance with his perfect, divine will. Paul likewise went beyond this and affirmed, "It is a trustworthy statement: if any man aspires to the office of overseer, it is a fine work he desires to do" (1 Tim 3:1).

Paul did not aspire to be an apostle; he was chosen and given by Christ. I did not aspire to be a pastor. I believe I was called into full-time ministry. This statement may make you nervous. Don't worry—I don't claim to receive revelation directly from the Lord Jesus. As a pastor/teacher, my role is the same as all genuine undershepherds of God's flock, which is to explain what God has already revealed in the Scriptures.

No biblical passage I know of teaches that anyone can "aspire" to be a gift from Jesus as an apostle, prophet, evangelist, or pastor/teacher. Passages such as James 3:1 and Hebrews 5:12 are not counterexamples; instead, they bolster the understanding that the body in general is expected to grow up and possibly teach and lead.[349] Jesus sovereignly gives apostles, prophets,

---

[348] Matt 26:31; Mark 14:27; John 10:11–16; Heb 13:20; 1 Pet 2:25. In Peter's epistle, Jesus is referred to as the Pastor (ποιμήν, *poimēn*) and the Overseer/bishop (ἐπίσκοπος, *episkopos*) of our souls.

[349] There is a difference between spiritual gifts and natural talents. In the same way, some teachers are gifted by God and others are capable simply based on spiritual maturity. Related examples are that all Christians are commanded to be

evangelists, and pastor/teachers according to his will and purposes. As these gifts are properly functioning in the church, we should see the saints growing to full maturity because this is why Jesus gave them. The "teachers" described in 1 Corinthians 12:28 would comprise those given by Christ as evangelists and pastor/teachers in addition to all those who grow to become teachers.

Leadership need not be restricted to those whose full-time work is leadership in the church. Elders and deacons should be appointed based on spiritual qualifications, Christian maturity, and the needs of the local body. Philip was a deacon before he was an evangelist. The church in Jerusalem had adequate leadership, so Philip was sovereignly moved to Caesarea before being established as the evangelist there. As the church spread to Caesarea from Jerusalem, God provided appropriate leadership to oversee his body.

If evangelists are rightly included in the office of elder as important and indispensable overseers who complement and balance the pastor/teacher function in the eldership, we can further understand the dangers of moving beyond the plurality of elders to a singular elder.[350] Biblically speaking, there can be more than two elders/overseers, but there should never be fewer. Therefore, the historical shift that began with Ignatius and culminated in the papacy in the Roman Catholic Church exemplifies the dangers of moving beyond Christ's design.

Some point to Ignatius's writings as proof that the singular elder or bishop over a local church was an acceptable practice that arose very early in church history. However, Selby accurately stated,

> Those promoting a monepiscopal form of ecclesial polity cannot baldly assert its historical precedence over the model of a plurality of leaders because we find the latter

---

generous, but only some possess the gift of giving; all Christians are commanded to be hospitable, but not all possess the gift of hospitality; and all Christians are commanded to serve, but not all possess the gift of service.

[350] Geisler discussed some benefits of a plurality of elders and an autonomous local church government and how this relates to both the nature of God and the nature of Man in his *Systematic Theology*, 4:124–28. Viola and Barna discuss the damage to both pastor and body in the singular pastor model in *Pagan Christianity?* chapter 5.

[plurality] present from the church's early years through at least the time of Polycarp's letter in Philippi.[351]

While some may disproportionately weigh Ignatius's influence and stress his close ties to the apostles,

> Polycarp certainly has as much claim to apostolic lineage as Ignatius if not more. Irenaeus writes that Polycarp, whom he knew personally, was appointed bishop of Smyrna by the apostles and that he was especially acquainted with John.[352]

Ignatius represents an early deviation from the apostolic model for pragmatic reasons, which was not fully embraced by his contemporaries such as Polycarp. Despite being an early error, it is an error nonetheless, and it continues to wreak havoc to the present day on those who choose pragmatism because they recognize it is easier and more streamlined to have a singular leader than a plurality of leaders.

The Christian path is often flanked on both sides by error. For example, we have one perversion of Christianity that claims works are necessary for salvation (a heresy called legalism) and on the other side we have an equally deadly heresy that claims works are meaningless (licentiousness). The truth lies safely in the middle on the narrow path.[353]

So it is with church government. On the one extreme, we have the error of thinking there is no need for leadership or that everyone should be a leader. This is not the teaching of either the New or Old Testaments. Leadership has always been and will always be critical for the health of the body. On the other hand, we see the unhealthy concentration of leadership in the hands of a single human or a strict hierarchical arrangement that magnifies the humans and not the living Lord, Jesus Christ. This also was never modeled or intended in the Scriptures.

Ignatius's model makes perfect sense in our inherited capitalistic culture that recognizes the importance of strong leadership in building

---

[351] Selby, "Bishops, Elders, and Deacons," 81.

[352] Ibid., 80.

[353] See also Viola, *Revise Us Again*, 145–68.

companies. We intuitively recognize the importance of a single leader who makes decisions and leads the organization—the CEO, singular, not plural. Yet the church is not called to conform to the ways of the world even when those ways are "successful."[354] Instead, the church is called to submit to the singular leadership of the head: Jesus Christ, who has given some as apostles, some as prophets, some as evangelists, and some as pastors and teachers.

Many local churches today have adopted the CEO model following in the path paved so early in church history by Ignatius. The *episkopos* represents the senior, or lead, pastor. The elders are then the board (sometimes called deacons or trustees), and the pastoral staff all report to the senior pastor. In some cases, staff reports to an executive pastor, who reports to the senior pastor. Ultimately, the rigid hierarchy is still present, which funnels toward a singular leader. The apostolic model, however, knows of no such hierarchy. The apostles, prophets, evangelists, and pastor/teachers were sovereignly given by the Lord Jesus to form a plurality of leadership under the headship of Christ. The singular leader of every church is Jesus. When properly functioning, the office of elder is nonhierarchical. Each division of elder merely serves a different function, and mutual submission should be expected and practiced. The events in Acts 15 are good examples of mutual submission between the apostles and other elders.

There can be no doubt that the apostles held a special place among the leaders in the early church. Yet even the apostles submitted themselves to the local church leadership and appealed to the elders. Geisler summarized it this way.

> To be sure, the apostles, *as apostles of Christ*, had authority to establish doctrine and practice in the churches (Acts 2:42; 2 Cor. 12:12), and at times they sent their delegates to set things in order (Titus 1:5). Nevertheless, they respected the local churches' authority and leadership. This is evident in that, first, they exhorted the churches to "obey those who rule over you" (Heb. 13:17 NKJV), and, second, they urged the local church to choose their own

---

[354] E.g., Ps 73.

leaders (Acts 6:3), to excommunicate unruly members (1 Cor. 5:4ff; Titus 3:10), and to settle their own disputes (1 Cor. 6:1–11). Paul submitted to a leader of a local church to be baptized (Acts 22:10–16), and he was sent out as a missionary under the authority of a local church (13:1–2).[355]

If the apostles themselves did not reserve power and authority to lead churches autonomously, it is unwise for our leadership models to concentrate too much power into the office of one human leader now whether we call that person a senior or a lead pastor. The consistent biblical testimony is that there was a plurality of elders in every church; this was the apostolic model which we change at our peril.

We must wrestle with the reality that Paul's expressed theology to the saints in Ephesus indicated they were already operating under the assumption that Christ had given some apostles, some prophets, some evangelists, and some pastors and teachers for the equipping of the saints and the building up of the body.

The most compelling interpretation, which accounts for all the biblical data and which has the explanatory power to explain why we don't hear more about evangelists or pastors in the New Testament and period immediately following the apostolic age (because they were discussed but under the terminology of elders and overseers) is that evangelists and pastor/teachers were both given by Jesus as necessary and indispensable overseers of the local church—a model intended to endure for as long as the church endures. When we deviate from the plurality of elders, especially when we fail to recognize the leaders that Christ himself has given, the consequences are always negative. Always.

The unity to which the church is called is found in the gospel. Sadly, the modern church has eliminated the "gospel" overseers in our local churches (the *evangelist* is a term tied to the propagation of the gospel) and retained only the pastor/teachers. Is it not evident that the present state of the professing church is not unified since we have a church on every corner? Is it not tragic that we spend an inordinate amount of time trying to maintain our theological distinctiveness from the other congregations

---

[355] Geisler, *Systematic Theology*, 4:68, italics in original.

even when we acknowledge salvation is not based on passing a theology exam at the end of our lives but by our position in Christ? We flaunt our disunity before an unbelieving world by building monuments to our division through denominationalism and having different churches on every corner unbelievers pass on their way to the golf course. This is because we have pastor/teachers operating independently without evangelists.

While we divide ourselves over nonessential doctrines, the world is perishing around us.[356] Unless and until we take seriously the vacancy of the office of evangelist (and the reality that many local fellowships have false shepherds and teachers and spiritually unqualified elders and deacons), we will continue reaping harvests of disunity, immaturity, and a lack of love for our brothers and sisters in Christ and for the world perishing around us while we fatten ourselves in the day of slaughter.[357] If we have strayed from Christ's perfect design for his church and if we have forsaken one of his gifts for the equipping and edifying of his body, we must come back in line with his revealed will. Reform is possible.

A question remains: if this is all true, where do we go from here? This will be the focus of the next chapter.

Joel—A Testimony

(Joel is cofounder of Fourth Year Ministries and serves a church as an evangelist. He personally shares the gospel with thousands of people each year and equips and helps other Christians to do the same.)

It is good to begin by explaining our terms. When I speak of an *evangelist*, what I mean is a person who fills an office in a church as a leader. This office is one of the specialized functions of the office of elder. That is not to say that all elders are evangelists but that all evangelists (in addition to the other persons listed in Ephesians 4:11) are all elders who serve a particular function in local church leadership. Evangelists work with the other elders to build up and equip God's people in a particular church.

---

[356] Since I am a pastor, I understand that most pastor/teachers act as if there is no such thing as a nonessential doctrine, or if there is, nonessentials are always what other pastors are worried about. All our pet doctrines are clearly essential!

[357] Jas 5:1–6.

The church needs evangelists to train the people of God to do the work Jesus commanded believers to do; a ministry Paul talked about in 2 Corinthians 5. Without the outward focus of a church being maintained through the leadership of the evangelist, it will naturally become inwardly focused. This is natural because the pastor exists to care for the body by teaching, preaching, counseling, and loving with a focus on the people the Lord has brought to the congregation.

How do we bring people into the fellowship of the local church? The evangelist, with the help and support of the other elders, trains and then leads the body of Christ in local missions work, the preaching of the gospel in love by the whole body. This preaching of the gospel can happen in many different contexts and situations: one-on-one conversations, proclamations to large groups, conversations between people who have known each other for a long time, and with strangers we intentionally tell about the glorious truth of the gospel. The church exists to reach everyone with the gospel, and only when the whole body works together does this become a possibility. For the church to be healthy, it must be conformed to the image Jesus gave us in Ephesians 4, the way he designed his church to operate.

The church must be founded on and rooted in the Word of God, the foundation of the apostles and prophets.[358] With this first step understood and established in keeping with Jesus's teaching, a healthy and fully functioning church is designed to have both a pastor/teacher and an evangelist. There can be more elders than this, but it is unhealthy to have fewer than at least these two fulfilling the plurality of elders model established by the apostles in every New Testament church.

When properly functioning and working with each other, these two specialized elders will naturally continue the cycle of equipping and leading the body of Christ into the world, preaching the gospel, and baptizing and making disciples of those who repent and trust in Christ alone for salvation.[359] Once this cycle starts and is maintained, there is no telling how much God will do through such an obedient church. God is capable of doing more than you could ever ask or imagine.[360] It starts with obedience and ends with God's will.

---

[358] Eph 2:19–22.

[359] Eph 4:11–16; Matt 28:18–20; 2 Cor 5:17–21.

[360] Eph 3:20–21.

I didn't always believe in this model of church leadership. I also did not immediately understand the importance of reforming our ways and getting back to Jesus's design for his church as revealed in Ephesians 4:11–16. As God works in my life, I see the importance more clearly.

I grew up in a Christian home and had what I consider a relatively normal childhood. My mom was saved at age nineteen and my dad at twenty-three; they raised us to know the Lord. We went to church weekly, and my parents were involved in home group meetings. I remember always being a part of the life of the church. However, while I was growing up in the church, I never experienced any outward focus of the church. We had church picnics, parties, softball leagues, and other events of this sort, but I remember them being only for the believers.

The main focus of our church life always seemed to be about personal and spiritual growth of the believers. I must point out that focusing on the spiritual growth of individuals and the body is a great thing; that emphasis is biblical.[361] However, as we study the Bible, we see that a very important and critical part of growth and fellowship is missing if this is all we focus on. The church exists to make Jesus known to the world.[362] We are Christ's ambassadors (remember 2 Corinthians 5). We are called to bring the message of reconciliation to a lost and dead world. This external focus is an important part of our individual and corporate spiritual growth.[363]

I did not realize this while I was growing up because I did not see others in the church doing this. I was never exposed to the church walking in the ministry of reconciliation. The idea that the church was mostly for my growth followed me into adulthood.

Once I became an adult, I wanted to serve the Lord; however, everything I did or sought to do was still focused on the church and the needs of the body. I thought Christianity was going to church, being saved, serving the church, getting married, having kids, and teaching them to do the same thing. I stress that in many ways, this is the right attitude, and I am not saying we should not worry about the health of the church; doing

---

[361] E.g., Acts 2:44–47.

[362] Matt 10:27, 28:18–20; Mark 16:15; Luke 24:44–49; Acts 1:8; 2 Cor 2:14–17, 5:17–21, etc.

[363] E.g., Eph 4:15–16, 6:15.

so is a biblical concept.[364] However, I must also point out that the main ministry of a Christian is missing if we focus only on the internal.

All Christians are called Christ's ambassadors.[365] Not some. All.

In my married adult life, I became lazier and lazier about my Christian walk. I did not spend much time reading the Bible or in prayer. I still went to church every Sunday as I had been raised to do, but I knew something was missing. I did not feel I knew anything about the Bible even though I had spent the previous twenty-nine years of my life in church every weekend. My faith became more self-serving and self-centered. I looked at the church and asked myself, *What can this do for me*? *What can I get out of this?* I thought the church existed for me instead of understanding that the church existed for God's glory and pleasure.

This self-centered attitude was leading me down a path that was taking me further from God. At the time, I did not know what was missing or what could get me on track. It was not until the Lord woke me up to the truth of what a Christian was called to do that I realized what had been missing from the beginning of my Christian walk.

I want to tell you about my wake-up call. I was a business owner when the Lord called me to full-time vocational ministry. While closing a store that was not performing well, I became convicted that I was a lazy Christian. One day, I walked into my pastor's office and said something like "Pastor, I am a lazy Christian and want to get more serious about my walk. What should I do?"[366] I knew the answer; I just didn't want to do it.

His answer might surprise some of you though. He did not tell me to read the latest best seller or a quick fix or self-help book. Instead, he told me to read the Bible. I knew that was coming, but he challenged me to read not just chapters here and there but to read a whole book at a time in one sitting. He told me to go home, read Romans, and come back.

I read the whole book, came back, and we talked about it. He told me

---

[364] Gal 6:10.

[365] 2 Cor 5:17–21.

[366] My (Joe) recollection of this story is similar, but Joel left out my favorite part! After declaring to me that he was a lazy Christian, he said, "All I know is this: Jesus is the way, the truth, and the *light*." I said, "Well, you're more than half right … and that's a good place to start." I am happy to say, Joel accurately quotes John 14:6 today.

to go home and read another book (or more) and come back so we could talk about it again. I kept going back.

Paul's letters were just that—letters. They were not written to be read over a period of time or chopped up into bite-sized pieces separated from their context; they were written to be read all at once in their entirety.

From that day forward, I committed to reading the Bible. I began reading, and that led me to my next question for my pastor: Now what? I am reading my Bible every day and reading big chunks, but now what?

He told me I needed to start studying it.

"What have I been doing all this time since we first met?" I asked.

"Reading. Now I want you to study what you read."

This was scary because I do not like the word *study*. It reminded me of school. I was not too fond of school and studying, but because I had seen the growth in my life from reading, I decided to learn from him, and I began to study the Bible.

From that point on, I knew that for my relationship with the Lord to continue to grow, I had to dedicate myself to reading and studying God's Word through the leadership of my pastor.[367] He and I discussed the next steps in growing a relationship with the Lord. I had been reading and studying, but the next part was the biggest challenge for me. It is also one of the main reasons I believe the churches around us seem to be so ineffective. He told me I needed to obey what I was reading and studying.

Wow. Can I do that? I asked myself. I had in my head that I was reading in the Bible about "super Christians" who were sold out for the faith and did amazing things. I told myself that these were great men of God, not regular Christians as I was. I did not think that I was anything like the apostle Paul, who had been shipwrecked, stoned, whipped, beaten, starved, and persecuted. I also wasn't like others Paul had personally trained such as Timothy, Titus, and Silas who joined Paul on his journeys and went through a lot of the same stuff Paul did and never wavered in their faith.

This call to obedience of God's Word led me to look at my life and ask God what he wanted me to do. This led me to step into ministry as a youth pastor.

I had always had an interest in discussing creation and evolution; I was well versed in the topic. I had been studying Kent Hovind's materials for

---

[367] 2 Tim 2:2; Matt 28:19–20; Acts 2:42; Heb 13:17; 1 Pet 5:5.

years and had even developed a presentation using his materials. Since I wanted to use my gifts and talents to serve the Lord, I taught a couple of creation classes at my church. After one of my classes, I was approached by a woman who was helping to lead the youth group (our church was between youth pastors at the time) and she asked me if I would be interested in presenting the materials to the youth. I agreed.

We scheduled the teaching, and I soon spent four weeks sharing how God created everything and where dinosaurs fit into the biblical world view. Since our church was searching for a youth pastor at the time, our pastor was leading the youth group. He had developed a strategy to get ideas on what the students wanted to be taught and questions they had by placing a wooden box on a table into which they could put their ideas, comments, and questions. He would try to incorporate as many of the questions as he could into the youth group sessions.

During my four weeks of teaching on creation and evolution, the box started to have fewer sermon topics and more notes saying I should be their next youth pastor. I literally laughed out loud. So did my pastor.

I was closing down my store and planning on moving back home to the other side of the state. I still had a house there, and that was where my other store was that I owned with my two brothers and which was still operating profitably. But something started to change in me, and my pastor saw it.

Several weeks passed and the students were still asking if I would be their pastor. At that point, I even had parents asking if I intended to apply and saying they hoped I would. As the weeks moved on and the questioning piled up, I asked my wife, brothers, and my best friend if they could see me in that role. To my surprise, they all said yes.

I decided to have a meeting with my pastor to see if he thought I should apply. After a long meeting, I decided to put in my résumé. A couple of intense interviews with the elders and the congregation followed, and then I got the job.

The Lord took me—a formerly lazy, disobedient, and untrained Christian—and put me in a pastoral role, all as a result of my newfound obedience and personal training from my pastor.

You might expect this to be the end of the story, but it is just the beginning. My time as the youth pastor at my church was filled with difficulty and struggles as I started to discover that I was actually serving outside my call.

As I mentioned before, the students loved my four week presentation on creation science. However, that was a special presentation. It was developed to keep the attention of the audience, and that series took me many months to put together. It had visual aids and other props tailored for the presentation. I was not able to teach like that every week.

Most people find dinosaurs, the flood, and creation interesting because they do not understand them. It was also particularly relevant because most of our students attended public school, and they wrestled with these topics in science class.

However, I had not been hired to teach the students the nuances of creation versus evolution; I had been hired to teach the students the whole counsel of God, so I started studying and would teach on what I felt the Lord was putting on my heart for the flock of young people he had entrusted to my pastoral care. Over time, I started to see a pattern forming and so did my students.

Through my personal time with my pastor, listening to his sermons, and my studies, I found myself mainly preaching and teaching on our call as Christians to spread the gospel as most important. It seemed to hit me over and over as I read through the Bible. I also noticed a great lack of obedience to this call. It was obvious to me because I had been disobedient in this area for virtually my entire Christian life.

For the first time in my life, I became aware of what was missing in my walk with Jesus. Personal growth is very important. Obeying Jesus's command to go and make disciples is the main duty of all Christians. How could I expect to grow if I was living in daily disobedience of that?

The Bible is clear in teaching that we need to go and share the gospel with people. It is also clear that if they are converted, we need to disciple them. Part of the discipleship process includes teaching them to go and do the same.

I learned that this process had never been completed in my life until the time my pastor invested in me and trained me by showing me the reason I had been saved. God is building his church, and he uses us to do it. We are the hands and feet of Jesus. Our living Savior intends to work in and through us.[368] So we must get trained and then go.[369]

The more time I spent in prayer and study, the more I started to realize I did not feel I was serving in my giftedness or in what the Lord had called me to do. Fortunately, our pastor had set up a weekend evangelistic training class that Andy Lapins of Transfired Ministries was going to teach.[370] Andy is a traveling teacher who teaches Christians how to faithfully witness to nonbelievers. The weekend seminar was the catalyst the Lord used to get me sharing the gospel with the world. After the last class, I bought some tracts from Andy and went downtown and got in my first gospel conversation with a group of teens.

It was life changing.

From that day on, I knew what it meant to be a Christian. For the first time, I got to see the greatest message of all time work on someone's life. They did not become Christians on the spot, but I saw the Law of God open their eyes to their rebellion and watched them understand what God had done through Jesus out of his great love for them. I don't know if they are following the Lord today, but I do know they heard the truth of the gospel, and God can use that to save them.[371]

This newfound fire, this eye-opener, was what my pastor had been teaching from the pulpit for the last year or so.[372] In God's timing, the Lord chose to use Andy's ministry to set my heart on fire. That led me to focus on the gospel so much that it actually started to create problems in my youth ministry. Most of my students did not want to be told to share

---

[368] Eph 4:1–16.

[369] Heb 13:20–21.

[370] You can learn more about Andy's ministry by visiting his website: www.transfired.org.

[371] 1 Cor 1:18, 3:5–7; Rom 1:16.

[372] I (Joe) had also taught five different Way of the Master classes and several other classes on evangelism in addition to leading a small group on weekly witnessing trips to talk with people downtown. Joel never took any of those classes. Thankfully, the Lord chose to use an itinerant evangelist to finally push Joel into the front lines. Raising up a full-time evangelist for our church was much more effective in engaging the rest of the body than any traveling evangelist ever was (or could be) and was much more effective than my pastoral efforts to be both the pastor and evangelist.

the gospel or be shown how. They wanted me to talk about more "relevant" topics such as peer-pressure and more creation vs. evolution topics.

At one Friday evening service, I asked the congregation to pray for me because I did not think I was serving the Lord in what he called me to. Try to understand the situation fully: I was in church, with my boss (the pastor), and I was letting everyone in the service know I thought I was not supposed to be a youth pastor. I was not sure what I should do.

This led to meetings with the pastor and the elders to try to understand the situation and to discuss and pray together to discern what the Lord was calling me to do. It was during this season that my pastor and I started to read, study, and understand Ephesians 4 in a new light. We prayerfully discussed this with the elders over the course of several months before coming to the conclusion that there was an office given by Jesus for the benefit of his church that had been neglected for years in our body, the office of evangelist.

I struggled as a youth leader for about a year and a half because I had never really been called to be one. Those under my leadership struggled too.

Why had the Lord opened the door for me as a youth pastor? How did such an unlikely course of events take place? One of the most astounding things that happened during the transition into my taking the position was selling our house on the other side of the state. We were in the middle of the housing crisis, the bubble had burst, and I prayed and told the Lord that if he really wanted our family to stay where we were, he would need to help us sell our house. Our home was sold on the day it was listed.

The best reason I can come up with as to how such unlikely events came to pass is that Jesus wanted to raise up an evangelist for his church. Ephesians 4:11 explicitly says that it is the risen Lord who gives some to be evangelists, but his church was not looking for an evangelist; it was looking for a youth pastor.

The Lord used this situation to help our church leaders rethink what we had inherited as the model for church. Even though it was painful for all involved (really painful at times), what came out of it was amazing. Our pastor would tell you that he never even questioned if he should hire a youth pastor. It was part of the mandate when he was hired. Our pastor would also admit that up until that time, through seminary and ministry, he was never encouraged to look into whether there was even a biblical base for a youth pastor. Nowhere in Scripture will you see "youth pastor" mentioned, that is, anyone other than parents, who are called to raise kids to know and serve the Lord[373] and shepherd them. And they do not need a hired professional to do that for them.

The fellowship of the church exists in part to help parents raise their children, but they cannot do it for parents. Parents will stand before the Lord and give an account for their own children.

My transition from youth pastor to evangelist was exciting and scary. This lost leadership position/function in the church has become so rare that we could not find anyone in the area walking in this ministry or who could offer wisdom and guidance in implementing this in our church.

How was I to know what to do? Whom could I mentor under? With the help of my pastor, I had to answer those questions with the Bible and the Holy Spirit. Ideally, we would have these resources in addition to mature Christian leadership that had walked this path already. However, we realized most people think an evangelist is someone who travels, preaches at big events, and who does all the work of reaching the lost since they are spiritually gifted for that task. Certainly, ministries of that type exist, and I was personally blessed by such a ministry, but this is not the biblical description of evangelists even though it is a popular usage of the term.

According to Ephesians, an evangelist is a key leader in a church given by Jesus as a gift to the body who with the other elders teaches and equips the body to reach maturity in the faith. This leadership function was missing in every church I was a part of my whole life.

Why were all the churches so inwardly focused? Because they had only pastors. A pastor's job is to focus on the life and health of his people. However, this is also why so many Christians are not fully mature. We reach maturity, according to Paul in Ephesians, when our faith is founded on the apostles' and prophets' teaching (that is, the Bible), and then when we are under the leadership and training of the leadership Christ gave, which includes evangelists and pastor/teachers. Then, not before, we will become mature and will not be tossed around by every new doctrine.

We need to care about our brothers and sisters; we are called to help them grow. Part of that growth is going together and bringing the gospel.

---

[373] Eph 6:1–4; Col 3:20–21.

This preparation is the shoes of our spiritual armor according to Ephesians 6:15. You're not ready to go until you have your shoes on.

Since becoming a staff evangelist, I have trained many people. Unfortunately, not everyone was excited to submit to the leadership of an evangelist because many in our culture still believe evangelism is the work only of those specially gifted for the task while others believe evangelism is a secondary and optional ministry for the "outgoing" members of a church. Of those who willingly submitted themselves to my training, some have endured and others have not. Our main group over the past five years has handed out more than 100,000 gospel tracts in addition to getting involved in countless one-on-one conversations. Tens of thousands more have heard the gospel proclaimed in the open air at various events, gatherings, and places. In addition, we have canvassed entire neighborhoods with door-to-door ministry and affected hundreds more through outreach events held at our church.

The group the Lord has given me to oversee is full of mature, dedicated men who can witness to anyone at any time. You have had the opportunity to read the testimony of four of them in this book.

Their maturity is not simply measured by their obedience and preparation in walking in the ministry of reconciliation. These men can handle teaching the Bible and preaching on Sundays and at any other setting. This did not happen overnight, and it did not happen by accident. It was the result of their pastor and evangelist pouring into them and them allowing us to pour into them by submitting to our leadership given as a gift to them by the Lord Jesus as Paul taught in Ephesians 4.

Too many Christians feel unprepared, unequipped, and afraid to share the gospel that saved them; I meet them every day when I am out witnessing. If you are a Christian, this question is for you: What is the gospel?

I have a sobering statement meant not to make you feel bad or condemned but because I care for you. We are told to work out our salvation with fear and trembling.[374] We should always be examining ourselves to make sure we are in the faith.[375] If you did not know how to answer that question, how do you know you are saved?

---

[374] Phil 2:12–13.
[375] 2 Cor 13:5.

The Bible teaches that the gospel is the power of God for the salvation of all who believe.[376] If you don't know it or can't communicate it to others, how can you be sure you believe it? This is an important question to wrestle with.

My hope is that after you think about it and inspect the fruit of your life, you will find you are genuinely a Christian. However, if after thinking this over you come to the realization that maybe you have been putting your hope in something other than gospel knowledge, know that is a wonderful place to be. Your eyes are open to the fact you need to hear the gospel. Pray and ask the Lord to open your eyes and heart and read the next few paragraphs that contain the gospel message we hand out on our gospel tracts.[377]

Do good people go to heaven? The Bible says there are none "good" but God.[378] Answer these questions honestly. Have you ever told a lie? Ever stolen anything (the value is irrelevant)? Ever coveted something? (Coveting is desiring something you don't have.) Ever used the name of the Lord in any way other than to bring him honor? (That's called blasphemy.) If you answered yes, you've violated four of God's Ten Commandments. Jesus taught the greatest commandment was to love the Lord with all (100%) your heart, soul, mind, and strength.[379] Have you always sought God's glory above all else and obeyed him? Based on your answers, you have failed to meet God's standard of good. God created you and gave you life.[380] You rebelled against God and are storing up wrath for yourself on the day of judgment.[381]

The Bible teaches that it is appointed once to die and face judgment and that no liar, thief, covetous person, or blasphemer will enter heaven,

---

[376] 1 Cor 1:18, 15:1–2; Rom 1:16.

[377] We are so thankful for our good friend Marv Plementosh at OneMillionTracts. com. He takes great care of us and has many great tracts to choose from in addition to always working with us when we want to develop our own. They are a great ministry and well worth checking out.

[378] Mark 10:18; Luke 18:19; Rom 3:12.

[379] Matt 22:35–38; Mark 12:28–30.

[380] E.g., Acts 17:28; 1 Tim 6:13.

[381] Rom 2:5–8.

but hell will be his or her destination, a place of everlasting torment, the lake of fire, a place of weeping and gnashing of teeth.[382]

Whoever has broken even one of God's righteous laws will justly be found guilty and sentenced to hell for their crimes against him.[383] God is good and must punish all sin, but God does not want any to perish, and he demonstrates his love for us in this: while we were yet sinners, Christ died for our sin.[384] God put the punishment for sin upon the sinless Lamb of God and poured out his righteous wrath on the cross.[385] God demonstrated his justice for the whole world to see, and through Jesus you can be saved from the wrath that is to come.[386]

To receive this gift from God, you must confess you are guilty and deserve to be punished for your sins.[387] You must repent (turn from your rebellion and turn to God) trusting in Jesus's sinless life, substitutionary death, and resurrection on the third day fulfilling God's promise in the Scriptures.[388] Jesus is offering to pay the debt for all who will believe in him with his blood, and the resurrection proves only he has the authority to forgive sin, which no other religious system can do![389] He is offering you pardon. Repent today! Today is the day of salvation says the Lord![390] Read the Bible and obey what you read.[391]

I hope that you have a better understanding of the gospel and that you don't stop studying it for yourself as you walk in the ministry the Lord called you to as his ambassador.

These next questions are directed at those currently serving in pastoral ministry, however, I want everyone to think about and answer these questions while keeping yourself and your pastor in mind. Sometimes the

---

[382] Heb 9:27; Ecc 12:13–14; 1 Cor 6:9–10; Eph 5:5; Rev 21:8; Matt 25:1–46; 2 Thess 1:5–10.

[383] Jas 2:10.

[384] Exod 34:6–7; Lev 5:17; John 3:16; 2 Pet 3:9; Rom 5:8; 2 Cor 5:21.

[385] Isa 53:4–12; Gal 2:19–21; John 3:36; 1 Pet 2:21–25.

[386] Rom 3:21–26; Acts 4:12; John 6:37, 14:6; Ps 2:10–12.

[387] John 1:12; Rom 10:9–10; 1 John 1:8–10.

[388] Luke 24:46–48; Acts 2:38.

[389] Acts 17:31.

[390] 2 Cor 6:1–2.

[391] John 14:23.

best people to evaluate us are our closest friends because they can see our blind spots.

Do the majority of your messages focus primarily on trying to get people saved or urging Christians to get their friends, family, coworkers, acquaintances, and neighbors saved? Do you find yourself more passionate about the unsaved than the Christians you are hired to serve? Do you spend more time witnessing and doing outreach than doing in-reach? When you pray, do you feel more burdened for those outside the congregation who are perishing under the wrath of God or for those who are members of the congregation and attempting to walk faithfully with their living Lord and Savior on this side of eternity?

If according to Ephesians Jesus gave some to be evangelists but most churches do not have one, it is likely there are at least some pastors or elders who are serving outside the call placed on their lives. Some to be sure are serving in parachurch ministry. I was serving outside of my calling because pastoral ministry seemed to be the only option.

Most seminaries I am aware of do not have degrees or training programs for evangelists. By far, the majority of those who go to seminary get trained on how to be a pastor even if that is not their true call. That is a shame. It is a great disservice to the body of believers who are being tossed by every wave of doctrine because they are lacking a major teacher in their lives for the primary ministry of every genuine member of Christ's body: as an ambassador for Christ.

I want the church to grow in maturity. Based on the scriptural truth in Ephesians 4:11–16, I do not believe this will happen unless we do it Jesus's way. If we do not recognize Christ's evangelists, the growth of the body into the fullness of Christ will be hindered.

Please evaluate yourself and your ministry and ask, Lord, am I called to be an evangelist? This can be scary for sure, especially because it is so foreign to us in America. However, we cannot run from our call just because it is scary or unfamiliar. We can't run from asking such questions if we desire the body to grow to full maturity.

My hope in sharing my experience is to help free those who feel trapped in serving outside their true call. If the office of evangelist is for the local church to equip, train, encourage, and lead out, and if these men are given by Jesus to the church, then where are they? Where are you?

Hundreds of evangelists should be recognized and working in churches, but they are largely absent. Many who are called evangelists are walking in a ministry that caters to the lost through crusades when the biblical function of evangelists is to equip the body of Christ because the church will always be better able to reach the world than individuals will be.

If you are called to be a biblical evangelist, I encourage you to rise up, overcome your fear with the Lord's help, and take your God-given place in the church. If you are serving as a pastor, stop struggling to walk in a position you were never called to walk in. Seminaries, I urge you to look at Ephesians 4 and start training a generation of evangelists to work in the local church setting. We can change our church culture for the better.

Jesus is building his church with or without us.[392] We all want to participate, but we have handicapped ourselves by removing this important function of evangelist among the plurality of elders in churches. Leaders, I implore you to rethink the traditions that were handed down to you. Look at the biblical case for an evangelist and find one.

Pastor, it will be a blessing to the body and also a huge blessing to you. You will be free to operate fully as a pastor, caring for your congregation while watching them grow. You will no longer be trying to do two jobs. While you are counseling, training, loving, helping, encouraging, and doing the ministry you were called to, your evangelist will be leading the people out—the ministry of reconciliation will never stop because of a wedding, funeral, or counseling. You will also have a brother who cares about you and your ministry and will help keep you accountable, especially in the area of personal evangelism and staying faithful to the gospel. Until the time you are able to establish a leader in this critical role, I implore you to heed the command to Timothy and do the work of an evangelist until you have one.

God gave the evangelist a pastor, and he gave the pastor an evangelist. You need each other. Both are equal in the eyes of Jesus under the headship of Jesus with the other elders in the church. The functions are different: the evangelist focuses on overseeing the external mission of the church while the pastor focuses on overseeing the internal mission. Both ministries must not be short-circuited. The body must be equipped to make disciples. These

---

[392] Matt 16:18.

two must be in unity and working together. As my pastor and I can attest, it is truly a joy to have both ministries working together for the praise and glory of the Lord. That is not to say there are not sometimes struggles, but the difficulty is worth it because Jesus is worth it.

CHAPTER 10

Moving Forward

Unless the LORD builds the house, / They labor in vain who build it; /
Unless the LORD guards the city, / The watchman keeps awake in vain.
—Psalm 127:1

If we recall the power and influence of Paul's churches described in chapter 4, there is a vast difference between then and now. The pastor-only model of church leadership has proven successful at creating scores of passive Christians sitting in pews who observe the teaching ministry of the pastor each Sunday and who are largely left alone beyond contributing to the offering plate or participating in programs if they feel like it.

This is not what Christ envisions for his body. In this regard, the duties and responsibilities of the biblical evangelist may best be defined by what is lacking when the evangelists are absent from their proper place in the church leadership. My heart breaks for pastors who desire to take the work of an evangelist upon themselves as part of their lifelong call. They are bearing a burden that is heavy enough on its own already as pastors!

Timothy could do the work of an evangelist while fulfilling his particular ministry in Ephesus because he was not intended to maintain it for a lifetime. Pastors who seek to do the work of a pastor and an evangelist will usually do a substandard job at both. I don't say this to be critical but to be realistic. Pastors should be free to devote themselves to being pastors; their leadership team should include an evangelist who is likewise free to be devoted to his work. In this way, both are free to lead and serve the body in their particular callings. Both are blessed by the other's ministry. Best of all, the edification of the church and the evangelization of the world is unhindered.

I have seen the same thing played out in church after church—the pastor knows the importance of evangelism and understands the responsibility to evangelize and the call for the body to be equipped. Pastors know that "it cannot be the church without witnessing to all men about the gospel. Just as the body that does not breathe is dead, so the church that does not witness is not the church."[393] His strategy? Teach a class on evangelism. Then after the class is done, he teaches a class on something else he sees as needing instruction, correction, or encouragement. People in the congregation become aware of the need to evangelize, but often, very little changes and little to no real evangelism actually occurs. The body doesn't see it modeled every day. Sure, they can declare the importance of it, but it stops at theory. In some rare cases, evangelism will happen for a season before dying down because no one is leading the charge full-time.

Having an evangelist changes all that. The evangelist's responsibility is to make sure people move beyond theory into practice. The body needs to actually grow up into spiritual maturity and obey Christ's commands—to actually start speaking the truth in love. Speaking the truth in love is an important part of our Christian growth process: "Speaking the truth in love, we are to grow up in all aspects into Him who is the head, even Christ" (Eph 4:15).

Many professing Christians never experience this because they do not share the gospel in any meaningful way with others. In some cases, it is not their fault. Our church culture has removed an essential leader who would equip, empower, encourage, and demonstrate for them what this means and looks like.

Many Christians have been falsely taught they do not need to participate in evangelism as Christ's ambassadors. This sad situation causes many born-again believers to remain in a state of spiritual immaturity and needing to be spoon-fed by their pastors and teachers. Many Christians who feel they are not being fed hop from church to church to find something that will help them grow, yet they search in vain because they are simply being tossed to and fro by every new doctrine. What they need is an evangelist and a pastor.

---

[393] Lindsell, "Biblical Basis of Missions," 149.

Countless pastors are burned out and frustrated because the congregation does not move beyond its passive state into full maturity and participation in the life of the church. Often, these pastors blame their congregations. In reality, we are eating the fruit of our own designs.[394] We have eliminated evangelists from their place in the church and pushed them out into parachurch ministry. As a result, we have congregations filled with people who are not moving toward full maturity in Christ. The answer is not to blame the sheep but to look to the gap in the undershepherds and rightly recognize and fill this gap for the glory of God, the edification of the body, and the evangelization of the world.

Evaluating our present situation and attempting to answer the question, Where do we go from here? is complicated. The problem has been adequately identified—our church leadership is incomplete if it lacks both an evangelist and a pastor/teacher. Our leadership structures may have more elders than this (whether paid staff or unpaid leaders, with degrees or without degrees), but they should never have less than this.

But is the answer as simple as hiring someone? Maybe. But maybe not.

Remember, Christ has given some to fill these positions; we can't simply manufacture them. We may be able to get someone to do the work of an evangelist or a pastor on an interim basis, but that is only temporary.

This leads to another question: can we share Paul's confidence that these gifts from Jesus are already present in our local fellowships and simply need to be identified and established? Again, maybe. But maybe not.

Paul had a different context than we do. His confidence was well founded because he was evaluating the entire pool of Christians in an area. He didn't have the challenge of denominationalism we do today—a challenge we have inherited but also continue to impose on ourselves. In my city, when Christians gather to worship, they come from all over the place with little to no communication between leadership of the various congregations. Many who are fond of the home-church model see no problem with this, but when Paul wrote to the churches (plural) in Galatia, he wrote just one letter. When he wrote to the saints in Corinth and the saints in Ephesus, who likely met in house churches, again, he wrote only one letter each time. If an apostle wanted to communicate to the

---

[394] Prov 1:20–33.

Christians in your city or town, who would he send the one letter to?[395] You get my point?

Christians today are not united under a unified leadership structure. We must wrestle with the reality that many false teachers and wolves have arisen.[396] They fill pulpits and leadership roles in churches all around the world. Some fellowships have neither an evangelist nor a pastor, even some who may think they have both. Some elder and deacon boards are filled with businesspeople (some of whom are not even born again) who have been appointed because of money, influence, and longevity with no regard for spiritual maturity or biblical qualifications.

Trying to recognize the leaders that Christ has given is more complicated today. We have made it more complicated. It is certainly possible that you have the appropriate leadership lying dormant in your fellowship right now, active but not properly recognized. It is also possible that to find the right leadership, your fellowship should merge with another or perhaps even close its doors and join a church that properly recognizes Christ's appointed leadership.

I cannot claim to speak for Jesus beyond what is written in his Word. I do not pretend to have any idea how many genuine pastors and evangelists he has given us. Maybe Jesus will honor our current denominational structures and provide enough pastor/teachers and evangelists for every church, but I doubt it. My theology leads me to believe he has gifted his church with enough evangelists and pastor/teachers to equip and edify believers. It may require some drastic steps of unification under Christ's appointed leadership if we want to reap the benefits of his gifts. As did Hezekiah and Josiah, we have some stuff to tear down.[397]

Perhaps better questions are, What are we willing to do to ensure we are operating according to Jesus's design? Are we willing to merge fellowships if necessary or even to shut our doors and encourage our congregations to find the leadership Christ designed if it is not present in a

---

[395] This is a hypothetical question that posits an impossible scenario—there are no apostles today and the canon of Scripture is closed, so we should not be expecting any new letters. The rhetorical force of the question remains if you can get past the impossibility of such a scenario actually occurring today.

[396] Matt 24:11; Acts 20:28–31; 2 Pet 2:1; 1 John 4:1.

[397] See chapter 2.

church? Sadly, programs are much more important in many churches than is proper leadership. Many would rather have leadership that serves felt needs and rouses emotions than leadership that genuinely shepherds souls, nourishes spirits, and encourages growth in Christ's likeness. Many prefer the temporary fulfillment of lusts over the well-being of their communities and the souls perishing under the wrath of God. One day, we will stand before the Lord and give an account for our potlucks while the world perished around our perfectly manicured lawns and for not telling others how they could be saved through Christ while we argued with each other over which color carpet to install in the sanctuary.

Another question I hear often is: how important is it to call these overseers evangelists? The question is fair; this term is already loaded with meanings different from the actual biblical description.[398] It is difficult and probably unwise to be dogmatic concerning the terminology. The New Testament spoke of leaders and used *elders* and *bishops/overseers* interchangeably. There is no consensus as to whether this interchangeability related to the Jewish and the Gentile conceptions of leadership or if this is better defined as describing an office (elders) and a function (overseers). Both are possible.

Certainly, oversight was a function of the office of elder. In the same way, I think the office of elder is the catchall term for the leaders listed in Ephesians 4:11. So why introduce new titles in Ephesians 4:11 if these are all elders and that is the common terminology? These terms identify different types or categories of elders to distinguish their functions from other elders. While certainly not a perfect analogy, theologians are already familiar with allowing for different terms to be applied to the same category of being to differentiate function in discussing the Trinitarian nature of the living God.

While the term *God* denotes the Father, Son, and Holy Spirit, the function of each divine person is different.[399] To a much lesser extent, the office of elder can be the same overseeing office while having different persons filling different, well-defined, and necessary functions all while remaining under the same office. Therefore, to insist that evangelists are

---

[398] See chapter 8 for a discussion of the most commonly held views of the ministry of evangelists, which are all inadequate in light of biblical revelation.

[399] For a more detailed discussion of the Trinity, see Ware, *Father, Son, & Holy Spirit*.

their own office separated from the office of elder would perhaps be taking matters too far. However, if it is accurate that Philip was one of the elders in Caesarea, it is significant that he was referred to simply as the evangelist. When all the alternatives are considered, it seems that the best and most biblically faithful way to handle this is to understand that apostles, prophets, evangelists, and pastor/teachers are all a part of the governing office of elder, but that each term—apostle, prophet, evangelist, pastor, elder, overseer—could be appropriate depending on the situation and particular person.

What is most important beyond the terminology is the protection and administration of the function of each officer, in particular the evangelist for our present discussion. I suppose the work of evangelists could be adequately done even if the sign on the doors of their offices read "Pastor of Visitation," "Director of Outreach," or even "Elder of Evangelism." I marvel at the resistance to adopting the biblical terminology of evangelist. I believe it is best to redeem the biblical terms and roles if they have been hijacked by our culture rather than go with the flow of our culture and accommodate our practices to the times. However, as long as the function is recognized and protected, I am not willing to fight over any official title. You can call your pastors coaches or your deacons waiters as long as they are allowed to minister in their callings and gifts for the edification of the church body.

Whatever the eventual title, without recognition from the local church and a clear idea of the purpose of the leadership role, it will be difficult to be fruitful. Ferguson put it well: "One has to have the recognition of the church as well as the gift and doing the work to be a bishop, evangelist, or deacon in the church."[400] Without some formal recognition and establishment as an official leader, the ability to equip and edify is greatly hindered. We must recognize Christ's gifts and publicly establish and recognize them in some form in the leadership. Otherwise, the encouragement to obey your leaders is superfluous. We must know who the leaders are if we are to submit ourselves to them.

We must be careful to point out a related danger that persists when the titles offered continue to support the hierarchical structure of the monarchical bishop, under which all other elders reside. While we may not

---

[400] Ferguson, *The Church of Christ*, 297.

use this terminology, the model is the same when we have a senior or lead pastor and everyone else functions in subordination to this singular leader. Biblical elders were mutually accountable and in submission to each other. Peter and Paul were both apostles, yet they submitted to the decision of the collection of elders and apostles in Acts 15 under the leadership of James. Peter and Paul were both apostles, and Paul submitted himself to Peter's authority when being recognized as Christ's apostle to the Gentiles, and Peter submitted himself to Paul's authority when he needed to be rebuked for acting contrary to the faith by holding himself aloof from Gentiles for fear of the Jews.[401]

The elders in a church, whether paid or unpaid, should be on the same level and in mutual submission to each other as they all submit themselves to the head of the church, Jesus. It is certainly possible (and advisable) that the more administratively gifted elders—whether pastor, evangelist, or otherwise—would take the burden of administrative charge. However, this should not result in a boss/employee–type relationship. When this occurs, we are reflecting worldly rather than biblical standards.

Submission to each other should be exercised particularly in relation to the specific areas of oversight. Evangelists should not be attempting to tell pastor/teachers what they should be teaching and how. Likewise, pastor/teachers need not attempt to oversee the evangelist's oversight of reaching the community with the gospel. Certainly, if sin or false teaching is involved, it is a different story. However, when operating properly, each overseer should be allowed the freedom to oversee his particular area and be willing to submit to fellow elders in their areas of oversight. As evangelists participate in the teaching of the body and as pastors participate in the evangelization of the world, each is able to be an eye-witness to their fellow elders' ministry to evaluate and become aware of any impropriety.

In this way, no one is able to lord their authority over anyone, since mutual submission and accountability are built in as the body participates in fellowship and the life of the church. The evangelist submits to the pastor in internal matters and is edified and built up, while the pastor submits to the evangelist in external matters and is likewise edified and built up with the whole body.

This particular application causes many to stumble in regard to church

---

[401] Gal 2:7–14.

leadership. It is difficult to give up authority. Sadly, many ministers wrestle with pride; I myself am not immune. When I look at the apostles Paul and Peter, I see different backgrounds—Paul was a Pharisee with exemplary educational credentials while Peter was an unschooled fisherman, but they served the church in the same office under the same qualification as those appointed by Jesus and given for the church. I have a philosophy degree from the University of Michigan and a master's from an accredited theological seminary, while my ministry partner has no formal degree beyond a high school diploma, religious or otherwise. Yet we serve together as evangelist and pastor under the same qualification that we have been given by Jesus for the church. We began our working ministry relationship with me as his boss, but this was an error of walking in the ways of the world. We serve the church as elders and are called to mutually submit to each other and the other elders in our congregation while being held accountable to the body we serve. Our current structure is nonhierarchical; we submit to each other as we serve our church family together.

Congregations that genuinely consider recognizing an evangelist face challenges. First is the perception that pastors are all that is needed for the body. Since having a full-time evangelist as part of the normal leadership of a church is contrary to modern church practice, it will seem like a novelty to many church members. This perception can prove to be insidious and persistent even when the importance and function of the evangelist is explained patiently and biblically. Additionally, it requires bringing a new level of accountability and submission as the evangelist will be a leader on the same level the pastor(s) once occupied alone.

There is no denying the difficulty of this especially considering it will seem to be an innovation as this leadership structure is so infrequently represented in our modern experience.[402] This shift will take some getting used to for both the leadership and the body. Many members of the congregation will still want to come to the pastor exclusively, treating the evangelist like a second-class leader. This practice should be corrected; they should be directed to the evangelist when appropriate. The pastor must clearly communicate that the evangelist's vision and plans for the body are just as important as his own. That means the body cannot simply participate in the internal activities of the church and treat the external

---

[402] For a slightly different perspective, see Viola, *Reimagining Church*, chapter 9.

call as optional. Such an attitude is destructive, divisive, and detrimental to the health of the body. Likewise, the small percentage of individuals who desire only to evangelize need biblical instruction and to participate fully in the life of the body.

Defining the exact function and duties of evangelists is elusive, which many commentators have stated explicitly. Yet the failure to define every nuance of this role does not mean the responsibilities are vague or impossible to define. It also does not mean they cannot be distinguished from the other elders. The apostles and prophets were revelatory and foundational, but apostles were still distinct from prophets. Similarly, evangelists and pastor/teachers are nonrevelatory and continuing but are still distinct from each other.

Attempts to define the role of evangelists simply based on etymology have often led to erroneous conclusions. This is not to say the etymology of the term should be completely ignored or cannot help us to discern the function of the evangelist elders. Etymological investigation may be very helpful and insightful, but we must keep it in its limits. Any interpretation that attempts to separate evangelists from the church or from the equipping and edification of the body—attempting to separate them from the description in Ephesians 4:12–16 or from the examples of Philip and Timothy—are inadequate. The idea that the gospel is only for nonbelievers is false. Christians need the gospel to be lifted high in worship services, not simply in evangelistic outreaches.[403]

The gospel is the truth of foremost importance.[404] When Christians forget the gospel, catastrophe is right around the corner and the drift into moralism is inevitable. This is nothing new. Green wrote,

> The moralism into which Christianity tended to lapse in the second century has its roots in the New Testament. ... Very soon the Church became obsessed with subjects like

[403] Earnest Best discussed this in his commentary on Ephesians and in his article "Ministry in Ephesians," 154. Additionally, Paul Washer argued persuasively in the series preface of his Recovering the Gospel series that the maladies facing the local church today were a result of an ignorance of the genuine gospel among Christians.

[404] 1 Cor 15:1–3.

what was to be done about post-baptismal sin, and it was a short step from there to reparation, atoning for past misdeeds and the like, which came to its full flower in the Church of the Middle Ages.[405]

Likewise, John Bunyan's character Christian is seduced very early on his pilgrimage by Worldly Wiseman to abandon the path to glory by turning to the false promise found in Morality.[406] Though an allegorical tale, Bunyan rightly recognized that Christians and therefore the church must constantly battle with the drift toward moralism and away from evangelism. Having an evangelist who keeps the focus of the gospel in the forefront of the church is important. The gospel must be held high for the church and the world.

Pastor/teachers are not free of the need to keep the gospel front and center in the body; they can and must preach the gospel and teach its deep significance and impact. The gospel is the great flowing river of truth to which every other tributary of doctrine in Scripture is connected and is fed by. The pastor/teacher must constantly be touching doctrine to the gospel and demonstrating the awe-inspiring and comprehensive implications that the truth of the gospel has on every aspect of the Christian life. Doctrine without the gospel is moralism and deadly legalism. Doctrine empowered by the gospel is life and peace, allowing Christians to live obedient lives abiding in Christ as God produces fruit in them to the praise and glory of his name. As a result, the pastor/teacher must be constantly striving to unpack the glorious truth of God's person and what he has given us in his Son. Nothing is more relevant. Nothing is more important. Nothing is more precious or profound.

The gospel is simple. The gospel is deep. The gospel is the basic master course. The gospel is everything and the only thing. The body must understand these truths, and we must apply them rightly, consistently, and fervently. We must employ the gospel life among the body, and we must demonstrate the gospel life (through word and deed) in the world. The gospel is for the church, and the gospel is for the world.

---

[405] Green, *Evangelism in the Early Church*, 140. For more on the dangers of moralism, see Kohler, *Gate Crashers*.

[406] Bunyan, *The Pilgrim's Progress*, 26–30.

To be faithful to our God in his church, evangelists and pastor/teachers are both essential. Evangelists oversee the aspects of discipleship related to equipping and mobilizing the saints to proclaim the excellencies of God to the ends of the earth and to everyone in the community. Pastor/teachers oversee the aspects of discipleship in regard to protecting the body from false teaching and the correct interpretation and application of the truth for the believing community. Without either, our church ministry would not be balanced. We will be attempting to operate Christ's church without one of the gifts he intends for us; we will be trying to fly an airplane with only one wing. As a result, ministry will be hindered.

When it comes to teaching the Bible and raising our body to maturity, I have a clear plan. When it comes to reaching our community with the gospel, I'm all theory. I can give you a million different things we could do, but we'd just be doing a study again. (Remember, I'm a teacher.)

Not so with my evangelist. For him, everything goes back to the gospel. He's the man with the plan to reach our community. He's the one who thinks of every detail and who continues to get us past discussion and theory about evangelism to actually doing evangelism. My evangelist is the reason we've moved past talking about reaching multitudes with the gospel and have reached multitudes with the gospel of Jesus Christ. Having a full leadership team is also why I am confident we will continue reaching more people for as long as the Lord is pleased to allow us to endure in our community.

Perhaps the most important aspects of the ministry of the evangelist are equipping the body to speak the truth in love and helping them to grow to maturity in this area by leading and demonstrating how this looks in practice. Having knowledge of what to say and having someone take you by the hand out into the world and help you open your mouth and speak is incredibly important. Pastors can attempt to do this, but they can do so full-time only if they neglect their pastoral responsibilities. Thankfully, Jesus gave another officer to help bear the leadership burden and edify the body of Christ.

We can teach the specifics of our message, but without accountability, we are on our own to put these things into practice. Fear has choked out the life of many Christians and kept them from sharing the message of life with those who need it most. For the benefit of the body, I pray Christ will raise up evangelists to help his body move beyond theory into practice—until we all grow up to full maturity, attaining to the fullness of Christ.

AFTERWORD

But I have this against you, that you have left your first love.
Therefore remember from where you have fallen, and repent and
do the deeds you did at first; or else I am coming to you and will
remove your lampstand out of its place—unless you repent.
—Revelation 2:4–5

People I talk to about the importance of evangelists in the church sometimes get the idea there is nothing that can be done. We are too far gone, they think. This is the wrong perspective. It is true that if this view is accurate, we have drifted away from Jesus's original design for his church. As a result, if our task is reforming every church, I would agree this task is perhaps insurmountable in our generation.

However, the goal of our ministry[407] and this book is more modest than total reform of every church. Instead, the goal is to raise awareness of this vacancy of the evangelist as an officer for church oversight and to encourage churches to wrestle with the importance of this biblical function for the proper equipping and leading of the church. Once the awareness is there, it is up to the church leadership to decide what it wants to do about it.

It is amazing what only a few churches operating under the design of Christ can do for the advance of the gospel. Remember the potency of the churches Paul planted?[408] I would love to see every church turn to a more biblically faithful leadership structure. Failing this, I am confident that even one church that embraces this model will reach multitudes of people

---

[407] www.fourthyearministries.com.
[408] See chapter 4.

with the genuine gospel of Jesus Christ and will grow in unity, maturity, knowledge of the Son, and love for the brethren. I also know a church properly focused and oriented under appropriate leadership structures will enjoy far less of a burden than their unbalanced counterparts will.

I have pastored both with and without an evangelist. I could never adequately express the joy of pastoring a mature and maturing body under Jesus's leadership design.

While it is true the Bible does not give us a treatise on church government, we vary from what has been revealed at our own peril. When we understand that the New Testament documents, especially the epistles, were written often as applied theology, we will have a great context for better understanding the nature of the leadership structures that Christ has designed and not be overly dogmatic about our particular form. When each church operates autonomously under the headship of Christ, we see that each body is protected from the errors of other congregations and accountable to Christ for only its own stewardship of what it has been entrusted with. This is good news.

If you see the importance of filling the office/function of evangelist in your eldership, you do not need to convince the churches down the road to do the same because you are not accountable to them. If you have filled the office/function of evangelist in your eldership but your evangelist has different ideas and is differently gifted than other evangelists you may have heard of, likewise, it is not necessary to be dogmatic or judgmental in assessing others' ministries. To our own master we stand and fall.[409]

The church exists to worship God, to glorify him on the earth, and to be a dwelling place for him. When believers gather, we worship and are in need of instruction and edification. When we leave the assembly, we go in worshipful obedience to the command of our risen Lord to proclaim the gospel of Christ to the ends of the earth and make disciples of all nations. Every church is instructed by Jesus to have elders to oversee the ministry and edification of the body of Christ. Some of these elders are directly given by Jesus as gifts to the body to oversee the external (evangelists) and internal (pastors and teachers) aspects of church life. Depending on the needs of the body and the community, we can trust Jesus will adequately equip and lead his leaders to do what is necessary to complete their tasks.

---

[409] Rom 14:4.

We cannot dogmatically declare how many pastors or evangelists are necessary in a particular body, nor can we be dogmatic about the need for outside accountability and other oversight committees above and beyond the local church level. We can confidently assert that the plurality of elders in every church was designed by Jesus and established by the teaching and model of the apostles. After examining the alternatives, the best explanation of this plurality is that there was at least one pastor and at least one evangelist in each fellowship to ensure the work of the ministry remained balanced and ongoing.

In this way, the foundation of the apostles and prophets, with the continuing leadership of elders (evangelist, pastor/teacher, and as many other elders as are raised up and are necessary), was recognized and practiced throughout Acts as the normative model for churches. In certain cases, these persons may have been absent for one reason or another, but I am confident their work was being done until a leader was raised up to take the task more permanently.

In contrast to the apostolic model, we have inherited a CEO culture in the church that unduly elevates pastors to be the shepherds of the body; this is a direct usurpation of Jesus's role in the church! It is time to reform our ways and thinking and bring pastors in line with the other elders, both evangelists and general elders, as undershepherds in Christ's church to the praise and glory of his name.

Are we willing to reform our ways and allow Christ to build his church as he sees fit? If we are, we can share the apostle Paul's optimism regarding the church.

> Now to Him who is able to do far more abundantly beyond all that we ask or think, according to the power that works within us, to Him be the glory in the church and in Christ Jesus to all generations forever and ever. Amen. (Eph 3:20–21)

May it be so in our generation for the glory of our God.

BIBLIOGRAPHY

Books

Appleby, David W. *It's Only a Demon: A Model of Christian Deliverance.* Winona Lake, IN: BMH Books, 2009.

Armstrong, Richard Stoll. *The Pastor-Evangelist in the Parish.* Louisville, KY: Westminster/John Knox Press, 1990.

———. *The Pastor as Evangelist.* Louisville, KY: Westminster/John Knox Press, 1984.

Arnold, Bill T. and Bryan E. Beyer. *Encountering the Old Testament: A Christian Survey.* 2nd edition. Grand Rapids, MI: Baker Academic, 2008.

Barentsen, Jack. *Emerging Leadership in the Pauline Mission: A Social Identity Perspective on Local Leadership Development in Corinth and Ephesus.* Eugene, OR: Pickwick Publications, 2011.

Bauer, Walter, Frederick W. Danker, W. F. Arndt, and F. W. Gingrich. *Greek-English Lexicon of the New Testament and Other Early Christian Literature.* 3rd ed. Chicago: University of Chicago Press, 1961.

Beckwith, Roger T. *Elders in Every City: The Origin and Role of the Ordained Ministry.* Waynesboro, GA: Paternoster Press, 2003.

Best, Ernest. *A Critical and Exegetical Commentary on Ephesians.* Edinburgh: T & T Clark, 1998.

Bock, Darrell L. and Buist M. Fanning. *Interpreting the New Testament Text: Introduction to the Art and Science of Exegesis.* Wheaton, IL: Crossway Books, 2006.

Booth, F. Carlton. "Evangelism in the Home Church." In *Baker's Handbook of Practical Theology,* edited by Ralph G. Turnbull, 171–77. Grand Rapids, MI: Baker, 1967.

Bruce, F. F. *The New International Commentary on the New Testament.* Grand Rapids, MI: Eerdmans, 1951.

Bunyan, John. *The Pilgrim's Progress.* New York: Grosset & Dunlap, 1961.

Burtchaell, James T. *From Synagogue to Church: Public Services and Offices in the Earliest Christian Communities.* Cambridge University Press, 1992.

Calvin, John. *Calvin's Commentaries Bible Commentaries.* Grand Rapids, MI: Calvin Translation Society, n.d.

Campbell, R. A. *The Elders: Seniority Within the Earliest Christianity.* Edinburgh: Clark, 1994.

Carson, D. A. *Exegetical Fallacies.* Grand Rapids, MI: Baker Book House, 1984.

———. *A Call to Spiritual Reformation: Priorities from Paul and his Prayers.* Grand Rapids, MI: Baker and Inter-Varsity, 1992.

———, ed. *The Church in the Bible and the World: An International Study.* Grand Rapids, MI: Baker, 1987.

DeSilva, David A. *An Introduction to the New Testament: Contexts, Methods & Ministry Formation.* Downers Grove, IL: IVP Academic, 2004.

Dunn, James D. G. *The Theology of Paul the Apostle.* Grand Rapids, MI: Eerdmans, 1998.

Elwell, Walter A. *Evangelical Commentary on the Bible.* Grand Rapids, MI: Baker, 1989.

Elwell, Walter A. and Robert W. Yarbrough. *Encountering the New Testament: A Historical and Theological Survey.* 2nd edition. Grand Rapids, MI: Baker Academic, 2005.

Erickson, Millard J. *Christian Theology.* Grand Rapids, MI: Baker, 1998.

Fee, Gordon D. *Pauline Christology: An Exegetical-Theological Study.* Peabody, MA: Hendrickson Publishers, 2007.

———. *Paul's Letter to the Philippians.* Grand Rapids, MI: Eerdmans, 1995.

Ferguson, Everett. *The Church of Christ: A Biblical Ecclesiology for Today.* Grand Rapids, MI: Eerdmans, 1996.

Foster, John. *Church History.* London: S.P.C.K. in association with the United Society for Christian Literature for the Theological Education Fund, 1972.

Gaebelein, Frank E., J. D. Douglas, and Dick Polcyn. *The Expositor's Bible Commentary: With the New International Version of the Holy Bible.* Grand Rapids, MI: Zondervan, 1976.

Geisler, Norman L. *Systematic Theology.* Four volumes. Minneapolis, MN: Bethany House, 2002–2005.

Gilbert, Greg. *What is the Gospel?* Wheaton, IL: Crossway, 2010.

Giles, Kevin. *Patterns of Ministry among the First Christians.* Melbourne, Australia: Collins, 1989.

Graham, William Franklin, and John Corts. *The Mission of an Evangelist: Amsterdam 2000, [a Conference of Preaching Evangelists].* Minneapolis: World Wide Publ, 2001.

Green, Michael. *Evangelism in the Early Church.* Grand Rapids, MI: Eerdmans, 1970.

———. *Evangelism, Now and Then.* Downers Grove, IL: Inter-Varsity Press, 1979.

Grudem, Wayne A. *Systematic Theology: An Introduction to Biblical Doctrine.* Leicester, England: Inter-Varsity Press, 1994.

Guthrie, Donald. *New Testament Introduction.* Revised edition. Downers Grove, IL: Inter-Varsity Press, 1990.

Harnack, Adolf von, and James Moffatt. *The Mission and Expansion of Christianity in the First Three Centuries.* New York: Harper, 1962.

Hatch, E. *The Organization of the Early Christian Churches.* London: Longmans, 1888.

Henry, Carl F. H. *The Biblical Expositor ... With General and Introductory Essays and Exposition for Each Book of the Bible ... Consulting Editor, C.F.H. Henry.* 3 vol. London and Glasgow: Pickering & Inglis (printed in U.S.A.), 1960.

Hodge, Charles. *A Commentary on the Epistle to the Ephesians.* Memphis: General Books, 2012.

Hort, Fenton John Anthony. *The Christian Ecclesia.* Grand Rapids, MI: Eerdmans, 1996.

Hunter, Archibald Macbride. *Galatians, Ephesians, Philippians, Colossians.* London: SCM Pr, 1960.

International Conference for Itinerant Evangelists, and J. D. Douglas.

The Calling of an Evangelist: The Second International Congress for Itinerant Evangelists, Amsterdam, the Netherlands. Minneapolis, MN: World Wide Publ, 1987.

Johnston, George. *Ephesians, Philippians, Colossians and Philemon: (Based on the Revised Standard Version).* 1967.

Kaiser, Jr. Walter C. *The Old Testament Documents: Are They Reliable & Relevant?* Downers Grove, IL: Inter-Varsity Press, 2001.

———. *Revive Us Again: Biblical Insights for Encouraging Spiritual Renewal.* Nashville, TN: Broadman & Holman, 1999.

Kempf, Charles A. *Let's Have an Evangelist!* Greenville, SC: Unusual Publications, 1987.

Kittel, Gerhard, Geoffrey William Bromiley, and Gerhard Friedrich. *Theological Dictionary of the New Testament.* Grand Rapids, MI: Eerdmans, 1964–1976.

Koehler, Ludwig, and Walter Baumgartner. *The Hebrew and Aramaic Lexicon of the Old Testament.* Two volumes. Leiden: Brill, 2001.

Kohler, Joe. *Gate Crashers: The Offensive Church.* Eugene, OR: Wipf and Stock, 2015.

Küng, H. *The Church.* London, 1967.

Lange, John Peter. *Commentary on the Holy Scriptures, Critical, Doctrinal, and Homiletical,* volume seven on the New Testament. Grand Rapids, MI: Zondervan, 1976.

Laymon, Charles M. *The Interpreter's One Volume Commentary on the Bible: Introd. and Commentary for Each Book of the Bible Including the Apocrypha, with General Articles.* Nashville, TN: Abingdon Press, 1971.

Lee, Tim. *The Evangelist: A Vanishing Prophet.* Garland, TX: Patriot Publications, 1991.

Lincoln, Andrew T., David A. Hubbard, Glenn W. Barker, and Bruce M. Metzger. *Word Biblical Commentary,* volume 42. Waco, TX: Word Books, 1990.

Lindsell, Harold. "The Biblical Basis of Missions and Evangelism." In *Baker's Handbook of Practical Theology,* edited by Ralph G. Turnbull, 148–50. Grand Rapids, MI: Baker, 1967.

Lloyd-Jones, David Martyn. *Christian Unity: An Exposition of Ephesians 4:1–16.* Grand Rapids, MI: Baker Books, 1998.

Martin, Ralph P. *Ephesians, Colossians, and Philemon.* Atlanta: John Knox Press, 1991.

McGee, J. Vernon. *Thru the Bible with J. Vernon McGee.* Nashville: Thomas Nelson, 1981.

Merkle, Benjamin L. *40 Questions About Elders and Deacons.* Grand Rapids, MI: Kregel, 2008.

Metzger, Bruce M. *The Text of the New Testament: Its Transmission, Corruption, and Restoration.* New York: Oxford University Press, 1992.

Michelson, Dennis Lee. *The Biblical Origin and Historical Development of the Evangelist through 325 A.D.* Unpublished dissertation, 1978.

Mills, Watson E., Richard Francis Wilson, and Roger Aubrey Bullard. *Mercer Commentary on the New Testament.* Macon, GA: Mercer University Press, 2003.

Mitton, C. Leslie. *Ephesians.* Grand Rapids, MI: Eerdmans, 1981.

Moreland, J.P. *Love Your God with All Your Mind: The Role of Reason in the Life of the Soul.* Colorado Springs, CO: NavPress, 1997.

Nemer, Joseph S. *Beguiled by Brothers: A Healing Methodology for Pastors Who Deal with Betrayal from Church Members.* Bloomington, IN: WestBow, 2013.

Ockenga, Harold J. "The Pastor an Evangelist." In *Baker's Handbook of Practical Theology,* edited by Ralph G. Turnbull, 164–71. Grand Rapids, MI: Baker, 1967.

Payne, J.D. *Unreached Peoples, Least Reached Places.* E-book, available from www.jdpayne.org/wp-content/uploads/2014/02/Unreached-Peoples-Least-Reached-Places-Payne.pdf. Accessed November 18, 2015.

Rice, John R. *The Evangelist and His Work.* Murfreesboro, TN: Sword of the Lord Foundation, 1968.

Rinne, Jeramie. *Church Elders: How to Shepherd God's People Like Jesus.* Wheaton, IL: Crossway, 2014.

Simpson, E. K., and F. F. Bruce. *Commentary on the Epistles to the Ephesians and Colossians.* Grand Rapids, MI: Eerdmans, 1957.

Snodgrass, Klyne. *Ephesians.* Grand Rapids, MI: Zondervan, 1996.

Sweazey, George E. *The Church as Evangelist.* San Francisco: Harper & Row, 1978.

Sweet, Leonard and Frank Viola. *Jesus Manifesto: Restoring the*

Supremacy and Sovereignty of Jesus Christ. Nashville, TN: Thomas Nelson, 2010.

Thompson, Georges Harry Packwood. *The Cambridge Bible Commentary [on the] New English Bible.* [Cambridge]: [s.n.], 1965.

Viola, Frank, and George Barna. *Pagan Christianity? Exploring the Roots of Our Church Practices.* Carol Stream, IL: Barna, 2012.

Viola, Frank. *The Untold Story of the New Testament Church: An Extraordinary Guide to Understanding the New Testament.* Shippensburg, PA: Destiny Image, 2004.

———. *Revise Us Again: Living from a Renewed Christian Script.* Colorado Springs, CO: David C. Cook, 2010.

———. *Reimagining Church: Pursuing the Dream of Organic Christianity.* Colorado Springs, CO: David C. Cook, 2008.

———. *From Eternity to Here: Rediscovering the Ageless Purpose of God.* Colorado Springs, CO: David C. Cook, 2009.

———. *Finding Organic Church: A Comprehensive Guide to Starting and Sustaining Authentic Christian Communities.* Colorado Springs, CO: David C. Cook, 2009.

Wallace, Daniel B. *Greek Grammar beyond the Basics: An Exegetical Syntax of the New Testament.* Grand Rapids, MI: Zondervan, 1996.

Ware, Bruce A. *Father, Son, & Holy Spirit: Relationships, Roles, & Relevance.* Wheaton, IL: Crossway, 2005.

Washer, Paul. *The Gospel's Power and Message.* Grand Rapids, MI: Reformation Heritage Books, 2012.

———. *The Gospel Call and True Conversion.* Grand Rapids, MI: Reformation Heritage Books, 2013.

———. *Gospel Assurance and Warnings.* Grand Rapids, MI: Reformation Heritage Books, 2014.

Whitesell, Faris D. *Basic New Testament Evangelism.* Grand Rapids, MI: Zondervan, 1949.

Articles

Best, Ernest. "Ministry in Ephesians." *IBS* 15 (October 1993): 146–66.

———. "Ordination in a Church Catholic, Evangelical and Reformed: Ministry and Ministries." Mid-Stream 4, no. 4 (Summer 1965): 206–26.

———. "The Body of Christ." *The Ecumenical Review* 9, no. 2 (January 1957): 122–28.

Blasi, Anthony J. "Office Charisma in Early Christian Ephesus." *Sociology of Religion* 56, no. 3 (Fall 1995): 245–55.

Campbell, Alastair. "'Do the Work of an Evangelist.'" *The Evangelical Quarterly* 64, no. 2 (April 1992): 117–29.

DeJong, Harold. "Elders and the Work of the Church." *Reformed Journal* 15, no. 4 (April 1965): 19–20.

Elliott, John H. "Elders as Leaders in 1 Peter and the Early Church." *Currents in Theology and Mission* 28, no. 6 (December 2001): 549–59.

Glasscock, Ed. "The Biblical Concept of Elder." *Bibliotheca Sacra* 144, no. 573 (January–March 1987): 66–78.

Gordon, T. David. "'Equipping' Ministry in Ephesians 4?" *Journal of the Evangelical Theological Society* 37, no. 1 (March 1994): 69–78.

Hadidian, Dikran Y. "*tous de euangelistas* in Eph 4,11." *The Catholic Biblical Quarterly* 28, no. 3 (July 1966): 317–21.

Knight, George W., III. "Two Offices (Elders/Bishops and Deacons) and Two Orders of Elders (Preaching/Teaching Elders and Ruling Elders): A New Testament Study." *Presbyterion* 11, no. 1 (Spring 1985): 1–12.

Mappes, David. "The 'Elder' in the Old and New Testaments." *Bibliotheca Sacra* 154 (January–March 1997): 80–92.

———. "The New Testament Elder, Overseer, and Pastor." *Bibliotheca Sacra* 154 (April–June 1997): 162–74.

Parrott, Rod. "New Testament Elders in their Context." *Impact* 4 (1980): 27–37.

Pfitzner, V. C. "Office and Charism in Paul and Luke." *Colloquium* 13, no. 2 (May 1981): 28–38.

Rayburn, Robert S. "Three Offices: Minister, Elder, Deacon." *Presbyterion* 12, no. 2 (Fall 1986): 105–14.

Selby, Andrew M. "Bishops, Elders, and Deacons in the Philippian Church: Evidence of Plurality from Paul and Polycarp." *Perspectives in Religious Studies* 39, no. 1 (Spring 2012): 79–94.

Smith, Robert S. "A 'Second Reformation'!? 'Office' and 'Charisma' in the New Testament." *The Reformed Theological Review* 58, no. 3 (December 1999): 151–62.

CPSIA information can be obtained at www.ICGtesting.com
Printed in the USA
BVOW05s1721220416

445166BV00001B/3/P